STANISLAW LEM
AND HIS ALIENS

STANISLAW LEM AND HIS ALIENS:

A Tribute and a Challenge

Edited by

Elana Gomel

GUARDBRIDGE BOOKS
ST ANDREWS, SCOTLAND

Published by Guardbridge Books,
St Andrews, Fife, United Kingdom.

http://guardbridgebooks.co.uk

Stanislaw Lem and His Aliens

Copyright © 2022 by Elana Gomel and Guardbridge Books. All rights reserved.

Apart from any fair use for the purposes of research, private study, criticism or review, as permitted under the Copyrights, Design and Patents Act 1988, this publication may not be reproduced in any written, electronic, recording, or photocopying manner without written permission of the publisher or editor. Enquires concerning reproduction terms should be sent to the publisher.

Cover image: © Andreusk | Dreamstime.com

ISBN: 978-1-911486-77-0

The Vector's Dream

Back and back, we circle
to Trurl's bard. Poems, too,

require calculation, solving
for variables just beyond

our reach. Your life's sum
proves inescapable, shifting

borders and boundless threats
evaded by fragile verse.

You knew the distance between
stars is not so great — just enough

for prescient logic to slip in.

—AJ Odasso

CONTENTS

The Vector's Dream
AJ Odasso v

Introduction
Elana Gomel 1

<u>Part I: The Loud Silence of the Other</u>

New Worlds and Old Histories: Stanislaw Lem and Science Fiction in the Age of Disaster
Elana Gomel 13

Stanisław Lem's Atheism and His Two Approaches to Transcendence
Jakub Gomułka 23

Masters' Silence. Lem's 'Alienomorphic' Model of Communication
Jarosław Boruszewski 55

<u>Part 2: Science as Fiction</u>

Through a Mirror, Earthly: *Solaris*, Gaia, and the Search for Habitable Worlds
Emma Johanna Puranen 77

Reality as a Fluctuation, Reality as a Singularity: Between Stanisław Lem's Reception of the Universe and *The Investigation*
Filip Świerczyński 107

Literary Expressions of Nonexistence in Stanislaw Lem and in Italo Calvino: "The Third Sally, or the Dragons of Probability" and The Nonexistent Knight
Pablo Contursi (Translated by Romina Propato) 137

<u>Part 3: Fiction as Science</u>

Air Cows
Neil A. Hogan 159

El Peligroso
Robert Walton 207

The Prison-house of Language
Elana Gomel 235

Introduction

Stanislaw Lem has been called the greatest science fiction writer of all times (Westerby 2021). His legacy is unparalleled, both in its variety and its influence. He wrote classic novels of alien encounters: *Eden* (1959), *Solaris* (1961), *His Master's Voice* (1968), and *Fiasco* (1986).[1] Along with such writers as Italo Calvino and John Barth, he pioneered the postmodern techniques of intertextuality and pastiche, writing numerous reviews of, and introductions to, non-existent books collected in *A Perfect Vacuum* (1971), *Imaginary Magnitude* (1973) and others. In *Cyberiad* (1965) and *Star Diaries* (1957-1971), he combined playfulness and humor with philosophical depth, questioning the origin of the universe, the nature (if any) of its creator, and the fallacies of humanity. In *Summa Technologiae* (1964) and other essays, he developed a stunningly original philosophy and ethics of AIs, grappling with issues that our own age is only beginning to consider, such as the moral status of self-aware algorithms. And some of his ruminations on the Holocaust, informed by his personal experience of survival in hiding during the Nazi occupation of Poland, are among the most illuminating writings about this historical catastrophe.

And yet, those who know and admire him, are in a minority among readers of science fiction (SF). When you Google "best writers of SF", the algorithm obligingly presents the expected gallery of Asimov's and Heinlein's, none of whom, with all due respect, can compete with Lem's breadth of the imagination, depth of thought, and excellence

---

1. Unless otherwise indicated, dates are for the first Polish publications of Lem's works.

of style.[2] The situation is somewhat different in Europe. In Lem's native Poland, he is well-known, and last year, the centenary of his birth, Polish embassies and cultural centers in several countries, including Israel, organized events and conferences dedicated to Lem's influence on literature, cinema, science, and philosophy.

Still, there is something about Lem that seems to repel popularity. It would be easy to get condescending and argue that most Anglo-American readers are simply too stupid to understand Lem. But besides unfounded elitism, it is just not true that complex concepts or obscure style are unsurmountable obstacle to fame. Certainly, the writings of John Barth or Mark Danielewski (the author of *House of Leaves*) are much harder to make sense of than Lem's engaging and funny stories of Trurl and Klaupacius, the great robot engineers who once created a machine that does Nothing, or of Ion Tichy who did battle with his own Monday self. And while such novels as *Fiasco* are intellectually challenging, so are Neal Stephenson's *Snow Crash* (1992) or Peter Watts' *Blindsight* (2006), both well-known among SF aficionados.

The real reason Stanislaw Lem is still a minority taste has more to do with *what* he says than with *how* he says it. Lem's insights into the human condition, humanity's place in the universe, and the possibility of alien life are so uncomfortable and so contrary to the cultural mainstream that they are hard to accept. Unfortunately, they are also correct.

So, this book is both a tribute to the greatest science-fiction writer of them all (yes, this is my opinion) and a

---

2. https://becomeawritertoday.com/best-science-fiction-authors/ This is a pretty representative example of the many 'Best of' lists proliferating online.

challenge to all of us. The challenge is not to accept Lem's views. A contrarian himself, he would not appreciate a coterie of blind followers. Moreover, while many of his writings on AIs have withstood the test of time amazingly well, we now know more about computers than he ever did, and some of his ideas are outdated. The same is true about his cosmological and biological predictions. The essay by **Emma Puranen** in this collection lucidly analyzes both successes and failures of Lem's description of the extraterrestrial planet of Solaris in the novel by the same name in the light of contemporary knowledge of ecology and cosmology.

No, the Lem challenge I envision is to open our minds to the beauty and terror of the Universe in a way that enables us to question our most cherished assumptions and beliefs about humanity. The challenge is to seek disturbance rather than comfort; to reject anthropocentrism; and to go beyond what Nietzsche called "human, all too human". There are other SF writers who can offer adventure, escape, and intellectual stimulation. But only Lem can gift us with the pitiless clarity of vision in which we see ourselves for what we really are: insignificant creatures, lost in the vast, indifferent, and incomprehensible Universe.

In *His Master's Voice*, the novel about the failure of communication with an alien intelligence, the protagonist-narrator Prof. Hogarth describes himself and his colleagues, the cream of the crop of human science, as insects:

> *We stood at the feet of a gigantic find, as unprepared, but also as sure of ourselves, as we could possibly be. We clambered up on it from every side, quickly,*

hungrily, and cleverly, with our time-honored skills, like ants. I was one of them. This is the story of an ant (Lem 1983; 27).

In most SF novels and films, the Universe is trimmed down to our size. It is hostile or benign; filled with evil invaders or with friendly neighbors; it is our ally, our enemy, or occasionally, our victim. But it takes a very special kind of intellectual courage to remove ourselves from the center of the picture. And yet, without such courage, we are bound to be boggled down in the vicious circle of anthropocentrism. Paradoxically, accepting ourselves as puny insects may prepare us for the encounter with the inconceivably large forces that shape our existence. We are ants grubbing in the dirt but one day, we may grow wings to take us into the sky.

This book is not meant to be an academic analysis of Lem's writings. There are other studies that do that. Peter Swirski's *A Stanislaw Lem Reader* (1997) and his many other books provide a broad overview of Lem's oeuvre. Recent collections of academic articles published in Polish and German bear witness to Lem's popularity and influence in Europe (Friedrich et al, 2021). My own book *Postmodern Science Fiction, Alien Encounters and the Ethics of Posthumanism: Beyond the Golden Rule* (2014) contains an extensive discussion of Lem's major novels. Nor is it a collection of Lem's pastiches, such as the delightful *Lemistry*, edited by Ra Page and Magda Raczynska (2011). Rather, it is a series of questions, addressed to Lem's texts and to us as his readers. Therefore, it is quite heterogeneous. It combines academic discussions of Lem's philosophy; analyses of his novels and short stories; and several pieces of fiction, none of which borrows Lem's settings or characters. Instead, they attempt to capture the spirit of Lem's writings, especially in their depiction of the sublimity of alien environments, the difficulty of alien communication, and the combination of humor and serious intellectual content.

The book is divided into three parts. The first, titled *The Loud Silence of the Other*, addresses a central issue in Lem's oeuvre: the impossibility and necessity of communicating with the Other.

SF is filled with aliens fluently talking in idiomatic American English with the help of some futuristic equivalent of Google Translate. But we know that communication across cultural and linguistic fault lines is fraught with difficulties even within our own species. We cannot communicate with other sentient species on our own planet, such as whales, corvids, or primates. How are we going to understand creatures of a totally different biology and culture?

With some notable exceptions, such as works by Ted Chiang, Peter Watts, and China Miéville, this question is seldom raised in Anglo-American SF. But it is central to Lem's oeuvre. *Solaris*, his best-known novel, is about the failure of alien contact. The godlike Ocean of the planet Solaris plays havoc with the lives of the scientists who study it. Its motives (if any) are unknowable; its actions make no sense; and the creation of "visitors" based on the scientists' repressed memories and desires appears to be extraordinarily cruel. And yet, Lem's protagonist Kris Kelvin stubbornly reaches out to this inscrutable omnipotent force, even at the price of his own humanity. The essays in Part 1 address the literary, philosophical, and scientific implications of Lem's unique model of mis/communication with the Other.

The first essay in this part is my own "New Worlds and Old Histories: Stanislaw Lem and Science Fiction in the Age of Disaster". I analyze Lem's notion of the inevitable failure of alien contact in the context of our own age: the age of climate change, pandemics, and global forces we can neither understand nor control. I argue that Lem's anti-humanism is the only fitting philosophy for this age, because in order to survive, humanity needs to embrace the irreducible alterity of the universe and to transcend our own complacent anthropomorphism.

Jakub Gomułka's "Stanisław Lem's Atheism and His Two Approaches to Transcendence" takes up the issue of transcendence and the thorny question of Lem's attitude to religion. It ranges far and wide, referencing Lem's autobiographical writings about his Holocaust experience; his essays; and finally, his fiction, especially *Solaris*, which has been occasionally (and wrongly) read as a religious allegory. It is not that the Ocean is a stand-in for God but rather, that the characters in this novel are faced with something incomprehensible and vast that seems to play a cruel game with them but may, in fact, be simply limited in its understanding of humanity. From there, Gomulka proceeds with an in-depth analysis of the Twenty-first Voyage in *The Star Diaries*, Lem's most thorough and challenging exploration of the idea of a limited or "sick" God. The English translation of this astounding tale omits some crucial material, which Gomulka restores in his discussion.

Jarosław Boruszewski's "Masters' Silence: Lem's 'Alienomorphic' Model of Communication" delves into

Lem's unique notion of the laws of physics being the outcome of the "cosmic game" played by inconceivably advanced alien civilizations. Lem offers a totally original solution to the Fermi Paradox. The famous paradox asks a simple question: If advanced aliens exist, where are they? Boruszewski discusses Lem's solution as proposed in "Metafantasia: The Possibilities of Science Fiction" and developed in "A Perfect Vacuum" in the form of New Cosmogony. It is the idea of a Universe as Game, or more precisely, a palimpsest of games played by cosmic civilizations. In such a model, however, there can be no question of communication in the traditional sense. Instead of deploying transmitters or radio signals to send messages, players use laws of nature as their game chips.

The second Part, *Science As Fiction*, includes essays that consider Lem's contribution to the philosophy of science. It begins with **Emma Johanna Puranen's** essay "Through a Mirror, Earthly: *Solaris*, Gaia, and the Search for Habitable Worlds" which places *Solaris* in the context of our contemporary exploration of exo-planets and of the Gaia Hypothesis which sees the Earth as a self-regulating superorganism. Fascinating, erudite and topical, this essay would make those SF fans who are unfortunately familiar with *Solaris* only through the lens of two very poor cinematic adaptations, want to read the novel.

Filip Świerczyński's "Reality as a Fluctuation, Reality as a Singularity: Between Stanisław Lem's Reception of the Universe and The Investigation" takes up one of Lem's most challenging ideas: that reality is purely stochastic, random, and unpredictable. This view is the opposite of conspiracy theories, in which everything is meaningful. Lem's novel *The*

Investigation (1959) starts as an episode of X-files, with a slew of strange events, including dead bodies walking out of the morgue. But instead of proceeding toward a satisfactory – from the narrative point of view – solution, in which all the loose ends are tied together into a neat knot, the novel becomes a narrative exploration of chance. It seems impossible to base a mystery novel on randomness, but Lem does it brilliantly (and repeats this feat in his later *Chain of Chance*). Świerczyński's essay discusses Lem's postulate of stochastic-fluctuating nature of reality with the help of the conceptual apparatus developed by modern physics. The essay is divided into two parts: the first is devoted to the idea of statistical *singularities;* the second — to the narrative use of singularities in *The Investigation* (1959) and *His Master's Voice* (1968). The essay gives a brilliant exposition of Lem's Universe – a place, in which "everything solid melts into thin air" and uncertainty is the only certain thing.

Pablo Contursi's "Literary Expressions of Nonexistence in Stanislaw Lem and in Italo Calvino" focuses on the concept of non-existence, comparing Lem's deployment of it with another famous postmodern writer, Italo Calvino. The essay does not stop at purely literary analysis but poses some tough philosophical questions. What IS nonexistence? How can we talk about absence as a positive force? Is God the Absolute Other precisely because He does not exist?

The last Part, *Fiction as Science,* includes stories written as tribute to, and inspired by, Lem's fictions. They do not borrow any of Lem's plots or settings but rather, try to pay homage to Lem's SF poetics in their own unique way. "Air Cows" by **Neil A. Hogan** is a delightful pastiche of classic

SF tropes, from time travel and speculative biology to alien encounters, set in post-war Poland. It combines sense of wonder with wry humor, much as Lem does in his many tales in *Cyberiad* and *Mortal Engines* (1977).

Robert Walton's "El Peligroso" is an adventure tale of mountain climbing in space with an unexpected twist at the end. Its otherworldly setting, its stark confrontation between a solitary human being and the uncaring Universe, and most of all, its evocation of the sublime, vividly recall Lem's *Tales of Pirx the Pilot* (1966) and *Fiasco*.

This Part ends with my own story "The Prison-House of Language". My own abiding love for Lem inspired this tale of an alien language and family betrayal.

—Elana Gomel

Part 1.
The Loud Silence of the Other

New Worlds and Old Histories: Stanislaw Lem and Science Fiction in the Age of Disaster

Elana Gomel

Stanislaw Lem died in 2006. During his lifetime, he witnessed the rise of Stalin and Hitler, World War 2, the Holocaust, the Cold War, and the collapse of communism. We are celebrating his work at the time when the slow-moving catastrophe of climate change, the global pandemic, and the war in Ukraine seem to be on track to make the 21st century rival the preceding one for the title of the *Age of Apocalypse*. But what, if anything, can we learn from Lem about confronting the apocalypse? After all, as a science-fiction writer he is supposed to look to the future, and his future is our present.

Stanislaw Lem is arguably the greatest unknown science fiction writer of the last century. On the one hand, his contribution to SF, futurology, and philosophy of science can hardly be exaggerated. On the other hand, despite the renewed interest sparked off by his centenary, he is not as popular among SF fans as many lesser writers. In 1999, a reviewer wrote in the *Vario* magazine:

> *Lem is...one of the most important European authors of his generation; yet he commands little critical attention and has failed to reach discerning American science fiction readers.*[1]

---

1. http://www.variomagazine.com/content.asp?id=16

Since then, the situation has changed for the better – but not enough. In a recent book, Peter Swirski, a prominent Lem scholar, still writes about "the failure to engage Lem at a scope commensurate with the level of his intellectual ambitions" (Swirski 3). He means specifically the critical failure to understand Lem's revolutionary scientific ideas, from his analysis of AI in *Summa Technologiae* to his use of statistics in *The Investigation* (1959) and *Chain of Chance* (1975). But I would argue that an even denser fog of incomprehension or outright falsification shrouds Lem's philosophical insights. And perhaps the reason is that these insights are extremely uncomfortable; and yet, they are indispensable if we are to understand our current predicament.

Lem was not a humanist. In his autobiographical "Reflections on My Life" (1984), he wrote:

"I began writing science fiction because it deals with human beings as a species (or rather, with all possible species of intelligent beings, one of which happened to be the human species" (12).

The "coldness" of Lem, often noted by critics, is perhaps the greatest obstacle to his popularity, especially in the West. We still believe that literature should be about "people", their deepest emotions, private choices, and personal struggles. And despite the ongoing philosophical critique of its tenets, humanism still remains the default stance of most public intellectuals in the West. The advent of posthumanism has problematized the single-minded focus on the individual but failed to dislodge it. Lem never called himself a posthumanist but his philosophical and literary explorations of humanity's place in the universe and its relationship with natural and historical forces are more radical than what most posthumanist philosophers today are willing to entertain. His response to the cinematic adaptations of his most famous novel *Solaris* by Andrei Tarkovsky and Steven Soderbergh is particularly revealing. Lem despised both films and savagely critiqued their anthropomorphism.

> *"Summing up, as Solaris author, I shall allow myself to repeat that I only wanted to create a vision of a human encounter with something that certainly exists, in a mighty manner perhaps, but cannot be reduced to human concepts, ideas, or images. This is why the book was entitled Solaris and not Love in Outer Space".*[2]

In other words, *Solaris* is not about the tragic love story of Kris Kelvin and his dead girlfriend Harey resurrected by the living Ocean. It is about an encounter with the totally Other – something that lies beyond our comprehension, our moral and emotional certainties, and yet perpetually challenges us to come to terms with it. The alien Ocean transcends our anthropocentric notions of good and evil. But unless we try to understand it by transforming ourselves, we are heading for a disaster.

In his book on the philosophical consequences of climate change, Timothy Morton describes our period as the time "when we are no longer able to think history as exclusively human…since in this period nonhumans make decisive contact with humans" (Morton 178). Climate change

---

[2]. https://english.lem.pl/arround-lem/adaptations/solaris-soderbergh/147-the-solaris-station?start=1

and pandemics are the result of natural forces that exceed our capacity to understand and control them. But similar forces operate in human history. From Marx to Toynbee to Huntington, philosophers, historians, and economists have insisted that individual choices and decisions are not the only, or the most important, part of historical process; that there are supra-individual factors, whether economic, ecological, cultural, or even statistical, that shape this process. These factors have always existed, but postmodernity has brought them to the fore. We are living in the age which requires "speculating outside the human" in order to survive (Morton 244).

In his critique of Tarkovsky's cinematic version of *Solaris*, Lem said:

> *This phenomenalistics of Harey's subsequent appearances was for me an exemplification of certain concept which can be derived almost from Kant himself. Because there exists the Ding an sich, the Untouchable, the Thing-in-Itself, the Other Side which cannot be penetrated".*[3]

Lem's great SF novels are explorations of this "Other Side", which we need to understand and come to terms with. But understanding comes with a price. "Speculating outside the human" means stepping out of our comfort zone. And once we do it, there is no stepping back.

In Lem's novel, the encounter with the Other transforms the self. His great alien contact novels – *Eden* (1959), *Solaris* (1961), *His Master's Voice* (1968) and *Fiasco* (1986) – are attempts to represent the unrepresentable, that which exists

---

3. https://english.lem.pl/arround-lem/adaptations/solarisq-tarkovsky

beyond human comprehension and mastery. They lie so far outside the cliches of Western SF that they seem to belong to a different genre altogether. Lem's aliens are nothing the malevolent Greys or cuddly ETs of endless alien-invasion movies, novels, and games. Very few SF movies or novels even try to present aliens as essentially *different* from humans. Notable exceptions include Ted Chiang's *Story of Your Life* (2002) and China Mieville's *Embassytown* (2011). But even in these texts, communication is possible, albeit fraught with difficulties and dangers. Lem's novels are about the *impossibility* of communication. And yet this impossibility is precisely what leads to a profound transformation of humanity, and the transvaluation of humanist moral values. The Other is silent in Lem. But this silence is more dangerous, more shattering, and more eloquent than the chatter of thousands of Star Trek "communicators".

Eden (1959) is not one of Lem's best-known or best-loved novels, though I have to confess that it is my personal favorite. It tells the story of a spaceship crew stranded a planet whose inhabitants are "doublers": obligate symbionts composed of two linked but distinct creatures. Their strange physiology is magnified by the strangeness of their civilization, which appears to have gone off the rails, producing mass graves, self-policing communities, cities where pedestrians are randomly executed, and mutilated, artificially distorted bodies.

At the end, there is an attempt at communication between a suicidal doubler and the human crew. Mediated through the computer, the dialog is clumsy and frustrating, leaving the humans wondering whether they are actually communicating with their own software rather than with the alien. What they glean from this dialog is a picture of a civilization engaged in some vast project of social bioengineering whose ends are unclear and whose means are atrocious. Written in the aftermath of the Holocaust and Stalin's Terror, *Eden* evokes painful contemporary realities in its unsparing depictions of concentration camps, self-policing penal colonies, and factories that recycle their own products.

And yet, the well-meaning humans decide to leave the planet without offering any help to the victims. The Captain (the characters in the novel have no names and are designated by their professional roles) explains this decision when the indignant Engineer insist that they must destroy the planet's government. The Captain asks whether they should have

> *"'Liberated the population by force?'*
> *'If there was no other way.'*
> *'In the first place,* **these are not human beings.** *Remember, you spoke only with the computer, and therefore understand the doublers no better than it does. Second, no one imposed all this upon them…They themselves…'*
> *'If you use this argument, then there is nothing, nothing that should be done!' shouted the Engineer.*
> *'How else can it be?"* (259; emphasis mine).

It is not that the Captain thinks that concentration camps are a good thing. He abhors what they witnessed on the planet. But at the same time, he realizes that human morality is not applicable to creatures who are not human. Eden, like its namesake before the Fall, lies beyond our knowledge of good and evil. It is a hard lesson to take in, but its relevance has only grown in the years since the novel's publication, with the well-meaning attempts to impose our values on other cultures invariably ending in disaster.

Solaris (1961) is Lem's best-known novel. Unfortunately, as I pointed out, it owes most of its popular recognition to its cinematic distortions by Tarkovsky and Soderbergh. Lem's irate response to both is actually more illuminating than the movies themselves.

The "Other Side" is this novel is the living Ocean – impenetrable, unfathomable, majestic, and silent. Compared to it, the doublers are as homely as your next-door-neighbor. Human contact with the Ocean is only possible through mediation. Harey, an Ocean-created simulacrum of Kris Kelvin's dead girlfriend, is neither human nor alien but both; and with her appearance, it seems some form of understanding might take place.

But if communication is the exchange of messages, what message does Harey represent? Is she a gift from the Ocean or a cruel taunt; a torture or a blessing? When Kris beams his neural recording to the Ocean, he hopes for Harey to be released from her bondage to the Ocean, so they can be together. Instead, she kills herself and a substitute Harey does not come back as she did before. Did the Ocean cruelly deny Kelvin's request, or did it give him what he secretly wanted? We don't know, and neither does Kelvin himself.

His Master's Voice (1968) and *Fiasco* (1986) go even beyond *Solaris* in undercutting any sort of communication or meaningful dialog with the nonhuman Other. In *His Master's Voice*, the unknown Senders of the neutrino message from the stars are as far beyond humanity as we are beyond insects.

At the end of Lem's novel, the project of decoding the

alien communication is an abject failure. It is even debatable whether the signal is artificial. Some biotechnology has been extracted from it, so powers-that-be are happy. But what does it *mean*? We do not know. And yet, paradoxically, the failure is precisely what transforms and ennobles Hogarth:

> *"The oddest thing is that defeat, unequivocal as it was, left in my memory a taste of nobility, and that those hours, those weeks, are, when I think of them today, precious to me" (130).*

Transcendence comes when we let go of our humanity, abjuring all our preconceived notions of us and them, sense and nonsense, good and evil. The silence of His Master's Voice speaks louder than the noise of SETI.

Fiasco is, undoubtedly, Lem's darkest and most difficult novel. Like the doublers of *Eden*, the alien inhabitants of the planet Quinta are engaged in what, to us, appears a shockingly evil activity. The planet is in the throes of endless war, waged by semi-organic technology, while the aliens themselves, of whose appearance we know nothing until the novel's last sentence, refuse any attempt at communication, responding with savage attacks to all offers of peace and goodwill. Inevitably, the human explorers who came to Quinta with the best of intentions, are sucked into the zero-sum military game of aggression and counter-aggression. At the end, the spaceships rain fire on Quinta, destroying what humans hoped to save.

Fiasco warns that anthropocentrism can be deadly. Trying to force the universe to conform to our notions of good and evil, self and other, will result in mutually assured destruction. In acting morally toward the aliens, the captain of the spaceship *Hermes* ends up committing genocide. As the priest Arago tells him:

> *"You wish to take upon yourself full responsibility. But in doing so, you have succumbed to the Quintans – by the mirror effect" (249).*

It is not enough to be broad-minded or accepting of the Other. *Fiasco* is about the failure of humanism as a guiding philosophy for the age in which "nonhumans make decisive contact with humans". As climate change and the pandemic show, nature is neither a benevolent mother nor an evil enemy; neither a helpless victim nor an omnipotent adversary. Nature is "the Untouchable, the Thing-in-Itself, the Other Side which cannot be penetrated". And while intelligent aliens have yet to make an appearance, we may be sure that when and if they do, they will be as opaque to us as ants, dolphins, or viruses are. And Stanislaw Lem is among the very few thinkers and writers who have had the courage to teach us this necessary, if hard, lesson.

So, does it mean that we are helpless in the face of the supra-human forces, be it climate changes of the black swans of history? According to his son, Lem was an optimist. His excruciating experience in the Holocaust left him not with despair but with hope. At the end of Solaris, Kelvin undergoes a mystical epiphany as he stands on the shore of the Ocean:

> *"This liquid giant had been the death of hundreds of men. The entire human race had tried in vain to establish even the most tenuous link with it...I hoped for nothing. And yet I lived in expectation...I did not*

> *know what achievements, what mockery, even what torture still awaited me. I knew nothing, and I persisted in the faith that the time of cruel miracles was not past" (204).*

In opening ourselves up to the nonhuman, humanity embraces the possibility of transcendence. In the age of the Anthropocene, we have to hope and believe that ours is still the age of miracles, no matter how cruel. Apocalypse comes from the Greek word for "unveiling". The end may still mark the new beginning.

Works Cited

Friedrich, Alexander. *Kosmos Stanislaw Lem*. Wiesbaden: Harrassowitz Verlag, 2021. Print.

Gomel, Elana. *Postmodern Science Fiction, Alien Encounters, and the Ethics of Posthumanism: Beyond the Golden Rule*. New York: Palgrave, 2014. Print.

Lem, Stanislaw. *His Master's Voice*. Lonon: Harcourt Brace, 1983. Print.

Lem, Stanislaw. "Reflections on My Life". In *Microworlds*. San Diego: Harcourt Brace Jovanovich, 1984. Print.

Lem, Stanislaw. *His Master's Voice*. San Diego: Harcourt Brace Jovanovich, 1984. Print.

Lem, Stanislaw. *Solaris*. San Diego: Harcourt, 1970.

Lem, Stanislaw. *Eden*. San Diego: Harcourt, 1989.

Raczynska, Magda and Ra Page. *Lemistry: A Celebration of the Work of Stanislaw Lem*. London: Comma Press, 2011. Print.

Swirski, Peter. *A Stanislaw Lem Reader*. Northwestern University Press, 1997. Print.

Westerby, Nick. "https://www.thefirstnews.com/article/one-hundred-years-ago-today-stanislaw-lem-was-born-he-would-go-on-to-become-one-of-the-worlds-greatest-sci-fi-writers-24688." September 2021. *The First News*. electronic. July 2022

Stanisław Lem's Atheism and His Two Approaches to Transcendence

Jakub Gomułka

Besides being an outstanding science fiction author and an insightful futurologist, Stanisław Lem was also a philosopher. He wrote four extensive essays (two of them, *Summa Technologiae* and *Dialogues*, were recently published in English) and numerous shorter theoretical papers. His philosophical interest covered in the first place, to no surprise, philosophy of mind, science, and technology. As a self-aware writer he also discussed problems in philosophy of art and culture. Much less obvious part of Lem's philosophical activity, given that he was an atheist all his life, is his philosophy of God and religion. This topic hardly makes its appearance in his theoretical works; instead, we can trace it in his theoretically-loaded fiction.

Lem's stories are usually very far from being just innocent pieces of entertainment. The writer employed his talent to an epistemic enterprise: he constructed elaborated thought experiments to "send a probe" to what is still unknown to science. By means of his creative imagination Lem tried to examine how a further progress of science and technology would affect society, culture, ethics, and our self-understanding. His science fiction narratives often served as means to put forward his ethical, anthropological, or epistemological views. Narratives employed to this task were serious science fiction novels but also grotesque short stories and bizarre apocrypha like reviews of non-existent books:

all these were utilised to carry on Lem's theoretical claims, although some literary forms were deliberately employed by him to weaken assertion of certain conceptions[1].

In this paper, I discuss central tenets of Lem's philosophy of God. My main aim is to show the two distinct approaches to transcendence that, despite not being explicitly presented by the author, can be traced down in his writings. I begin with a presentation of Lem's two ways of justifying his atheistic worldview; then, I go on to his idea of a "sick God" and point to its several instances in his prose. I put forward the view that the idea is linked to the "horizontal transcendence" framework; finally, I focus on the futurology of Catholic theology as presented in a short story titled *The Twenty-First Voyage* to show a different way of Lem's thinking about God that can be associated with the concept of "vertical transcendence". The sense in which I talk about the two accounts of transcendence and my use of the horizontal/vertical dichotomy will be elucidated in the course of the paper.

Lem's atheism

Lem, born in 1921 in a prosperous family of a successful Lvivian laryngologist, was a Holocaust survivor. His idyllic childhood and more or less carefree adolescence was interrupted in September 1939 as the Soviets annexed the eastern part of Poland[2]. Nearly two years later, in summer

---

1. Lem admitted this plainly, however he did so in a humorous text; thus, the assertion is deliberately weakened (Lem, 1983, pp. 3–8). Essayization of Lem's fiction is a complex phenomenon meticulously examined by Maciej Płaza in his fundamental work about Lem's epistemic strategies titled *O poznaniu w twórczości Stanisława Lema*, unfortunately only available in Polish (Płaza, 2006).
2. Lem's autobiographical novel *Highcastle* devoted to his pre-war life

1941, his life transformed into a nightmare as the German army invaded the USSR and took Lviv. The city, like all Polish towns occupied by Nazis, was generally an unsafe place to everybody. But for its Jewish community it was basically a death trap: of nearly 100,000 Jews living in pre-war Lviv, not even one percent remained alive by the end of German occupation. Others were killed in pogroms, daily executions, or in gas chambers of Belzec extermination camp.

Lem's biographers, Wojciech Orliński and Agnieszka Gajewska, point to several occasions on which the man who later wrote *Solaris* could have died, had he been simply less lucky. For instance, it has been disclosed that Rappaport's dreadful tale from *His Master's Voice* (Lem, 2020b, pp. 79–84) is in fact a detailed and accurate record of Lem's own experience of being a victim, fortunately not a fatal one, of a pogrom that took place during the first days of Nazi occupation of Lviv in July 1941 (cf. Orliński, 2017, pp. 64–67); (cf. Gajewska, 2021, pp. 126–134).

For a witness of one's whole social world being put to death, for a person forced to live undercover in a constant danger of imminent death when found out, it is very hard to hold the basic trust in the world unshaken (cf. e.g. de Warren, 2015). Without that trust, the Western metaphysical tradition of perceiving being as fundamentally good loses its charm

---

is saturated with the impression of almost paradise-like undisturbed youth (cf. Lem, 2020a). However, Gajewska suggests a much more nuanced picture: due to antisemitic sentiments that were prevailing among Polish academics in late 1930s it was not certain if young Stanisław Lem would be allowed to enroll to any higher studies, let alone his dream technical university. Paradoxically, it was the Soviet occupation that let him, like many other Lvivian young Jews, begin academic education in 1939 (cf. Gajewska, 2021, pp. 112–115).

and persuasiveness: one is more prone to see the universe as treacherous rather than benign and tends to think of one's own existence in terms of a curse rather than a gift. However, such a fundamentally pessimistic approach to reality does not need to result in atheism: many people believed in God in spite of, or even because of, the basic mistrust of the world. Stanisław Lem also did not give up his religious faith due to his wartime experiences: he was already an atheist before 1939. Despite having received mandatory education in Judaism and taking part in Jewish religious ceremonies, he lost faith when he was thirteen or fourteen years old[3]. Nonetheless, it is plausible that his particular experiences which were not shared by the representatives of Polish post-war ethnic and religious majority entrenched his unbelief. They likely made him immune to the influence of religious charismatic intellectuals, including Jan Błoński[4] and Jerzy Turowicz[5], whom he befriended after he moved to Cracow in 1946.

Moreover, it is even more plausible that the writer's

---

3. Or, at least, this is what he wanted us to believe (cf. Lem & Targosz, 2001, p. 21). Lem deliberately hid his Jewish origin and usually misguided his readers and even friends about what it had happened to him before 1945. However, as it has been pointed out by Orliński, he did it in a subtle way by using understatements rather than just lying (Orliński, 2017, p. 86). So, there is no reason why we would not take this particular confession at face value.
4. Błoński was a well-known professor of Polish literature at the Jagiellonian University of Cracow and Lem's closest friend and neighbour for many years.
5. Turowicz was the long-lasting editor-in-chief of the Cracovian Catholic weekly *Tygodnik Powszechny*, the only non-communist and semi-independent newspaper that was published in the Eastern Block before 1989. Lem was associated to *Tygodnik Powszechny*'s editing crew throughout his entire life and remained a columnist of the weekly until his death in 2006.

tragic wartime memories highly contributed to the shift of his strategy to justify the atheistic view that occurred sometime in the 1960s as he entered his middle age. A more optimistic scientific worldview he held as a young man evaporated, making room for a bitter image of the universe as a great meat grinder that simply cannot be a creation of a benevolent almighty being.

There are firm grounds for the claim that, initially, he appreciated the standard enlightenment anti-theistic argumentation that hanged on to the explanatory power of science. The main body of evidence is Lem's grotesque short story *The Twenty-Second Voyage* written in 1953. Today, the English-speaking public can find the story in a collection titled *The Star Diaries* translated by Michael Kandel in the 1970s (cf. Lem, 2016b, pp. 269–281). Alas, the translation is stripped of the very fragment exhibiting Lem's allegiance to the enlightenment anti-theistic argumentation. The translator loyally warns the reader that a few pages of *The Twenty-Second Voyage* original text are missing (cf. Kandel, 2016, p. 338); the omission is done skillfully and can only be noticed when compared to the Polish version. Interestingly, the decision to cut out the fragment in question was not made by the translator but the author himself. Lem, who could read English, oversaw the translating process and sometimes gave Kandel direct instructions. Particularly, in a letter dated April 25th, 1974, Lem recommended Kandel not to include some of the oldest stories to the English edition of *The Star Diaries* and went on saying: "I would remove at least the last few pages of *The Twenty-Second Voyage* so the piece would end with what the Gnelts did to Fr. Oribazy" (Lem, 2013a, p. 224)[6].

The short story describes space traveller Ijon Tichy's accidental meeting with Fr. Lacymon, a Dominican who is in charge of Catholic evangelisation in a distant region of the universe. The friar tells the protagonist about the difficulties his missionaries encounter as they try to disseminate faith among various intelligent inhabitants of remote planets. Lem brings about comic effects by juxtaposing the pursuit of individual salvation with the commandment to love your neighbour (hence the unfortunate fate of the said Fr. Oribazy tortured and brutally killed by newly converted avuncular Gnelts who wanted to make him a saint) and the Catholic claim to universalism with its entanglement in Homo Sapiens' random local physiology. However, the pages cut out from English edition introduce a slightly different theme: Tichy is told that one of space peoples within the mission area, a highly developed civilization of non-believers, turns out to be totally immune to any attempt at religious conversion. Church envoys suffer a complete debacle: not only they fail to convince those aliens but also lose their own faith and become atheists themselves. Although the Vatican, assisted by US professionals, produces fake evidence to prove that the atheisation of its missionaries is carried out by tortures, hypnosis, and brainwashing, the reality, as Fr. Lacymon sadly admits, is much grimmer: "They do not torture, force you to anything, nor they screw bolts into your head. Instead, they simply teach you what the Universe is, where the life came from, how the consciousness awakes, and how to apply science to daily life. They can prove as

---

6. This, and all subsequent quotations from sources in Polish, have been translated to English by myself.

clearly as two plus two yields four that the whole world is purely material" (Lem, 2008, p. 238). It is revealed that the furthest the allegedly sinister space atheists go on is to send a mystic nun to psychotherapy by gardening and playing with dolls.

The message behind this piece of fiction is quite clear: religion and faith in God results from false beliefs about the world and deficiency of intellectual maturity that can be made up for as we provide the believers with reliable scientific knowledge. That is the core of the creed of enlightenment atheism. Although it has been written in times of the greatest intensity of ideological pressure on Polish writers, there is no reason to claim that *The Twenty-Second Voyage* was merely a homage paid by Lem to decreed socialist realism style. Plausibly, it was a sincere expression of his own views at the time. Had it not been so, he would not utilise it to tease his religious friends as he used to[7]. Moreover, on the threshold of the 21st century the author interviewed about his literary works did not distance himself from the short story, nor did he criticise it but quite aptly pointed to its affiliation to the tradition of Voltairean philosophical fiction (Lem, 2000, p. 121).

However, the fact that Lem nevertheless decided to exclude the tale about space atheists from the English version of the story is, to say the least, intriguing. What was his reason to do that? Actually, more than one reason can be pointed out. Firstly, as late as in 1974, the author had another powerful strategy of argumentation in favour of atheism in his disposal. It had gradually gained its shape in the course of

---

[7]. I have been told about that by Wojciech Zemek who was the Lem's secretary during the last few decades of his life.

the 1960s, apparently as a side-effect of Lem's considerations of problems in futurology and the philosophy of biology.

Let us look into *Summa Technologiae*, the second of his four great essays, devoted to possible furthest developments of technology and their ramifications, first published in 1964. The eighth chapter of the book discusses the ways in which next generations of humans would reshape their own bodies through a scientific project called auto-evolution. The premise behind the whole idea is the observation that the actual biological nature of Homo Sapiens is flawed: the existence of diaphragm severely hinders the act of childbirth, upright posture causes varicose veins, the construction of human throat resulting from rapid expansion of brainpan puts people at risk of various infections, etc. (Lem, 2013b, pp. 304–305). There are also more general imperfections like fragility, ageing, and, last but not least, mortality. Lem does not merely affirm this but goes on to discuss why it is so. He notices that from a designer's point of view, natural evolution as a process of creating organisms is very ineffective and burdened with many disadvantages. However, his complaints come in hand with praises and, though the chapter is titled "A Lampoon of Evolution," the writer admits that the lampooning is not quite serious. It serves to signal that our scientifically guided technology has the potential not only to catch up the nature but also to exceed its perfection (cf. Lem, 2013b, p. 25).

Nevertheless, from the mid-1960s, criticism of evolution became one of Lem's recurring themes. The author underlined both biological imperfections of human and other forms of life as the opportunism of the very mechanism of evolutionary shaping of new species. They were products of "a billion-year process of ad hoc accommodations" that results in countless poorly patched defects (Lem, 1983, p. 134). No wonder, because biological organisms, let alone their wellbeing, have never been objectives of the whole circulation of living matter. Frankly speaking, since the evolution cannot think and make plans, it has never had any objectives, except for the circulation itself, that is, the constant transmission of the genetic code. Everything else, all the piles of flesh and stretched over eons misery of living creatures has only served to protect and duplicate the code (cf. Lem, 1985, pp. 138–153)[8]. However, tremendous cruelties of terrestrial biological evolution and its excessive superfluousness is not an exception to cosmic order. On the contrary, it is the very embodiment of one of the fundamental laws of the known universe: entropy of an isolated dynamic system cannot decrease. Lem, when interviewed in the beginning of the 1980s, said: "It is easier to shatter any object than to rebuild it: this is the entropy arrow, the second law of thermodynamics! It is not a result of one value system or another: it happens within every culture! This is space data" (Bereś & Lem, 1987, p. 397). Hence, evil is not simply a lack of being as generations of Western metaphysicians wanted us to believe (cf. Bereś & Lem, 1987, p. 372); it results from the core principles of the universe, it makes up

---

8. In the first of the two lectures of Golem XIV, Lem presents a view on biological evolution as governed by the three following laws: the meaning of the transmitter is the transmission, species emerge from errant error, the construction is less perfect than what what constructs (Lem, 1985, pp. 143–144). It is worth noticing that the publication of this Lem's piece (1973) preceded Dawkins' *Selfish Gene* (1976) by three years, although the gene-centred view of evolution was introduced earlier, most prominently by George C. Williams in his 1966 classic book *Adaptation and Natural Selection*.

the backbone of reality[9]. The world we live in is a Holocaust as the author recapitulated in the title of one if his 1980s' essays[10]. And it is obvious that the Holocaust-world cannot be a product of the almighty and benevolent creator. The writer went on saying that "this tremendous redundancy of the creation, destructive character of all stellar transformations, these hecatombs of corpses that constitute evolution is incompatible with any decent intention. This contradictoriness is incompatible with any sort of theogony and theodicy" (Bereś & Lem, 1987, p. 301).

The second plausible reason why Lem decided to censor the English translation of *The Twenty-Second Voyage* was that by the 1970s he was already fully aware that his previous Enlightenment-inspired view of religion, even if there is truth to it[11], does not give justice to the phenomenon as a whole

---

9. Lem points out that another aspect of the same merciless structural cruelty of the world is the fate of civilisations created by intelligent beings. It seems that at least from the 1980s he is more and more convinced that the process of technological development ends with self-annihilation (cf. Bereś & Lem, 1987, p. 298). Since "this world consists in great part of lunatics and idiots and its fate depends greatly on those idiots" (*ibidem*, p. 271) and technology provides us with advanced weapons of mass destruction, the prospects of human civilisation are bleak. Lem is aware that this can be a space constant too. He is one of the people who treat this as a possible solution to the Fermi paradox, that is, the lack of any observational evidence of extraterrestrial civilisations despite relatively high estimates of their existence.
10. In its original Polish version, the exact title is half-German, half-English: "Das creative Vernichtungsprinzip. The World as Holocaust" (Lem, 2009a, pp. 143–173). Strangely enough, the translator to English, for an unknown reason, decided to weaken the title's expressive power and changed it to "The World as Cataclysm" (cf. Lem, 1991, pp. 69–102).
11. One can notice that Lem continues his mockery of theodicy in his 1979 short story *Powtórka* (Lem, 2015, pp. 426–434).

and therefore the latter cannot be simply dispelled by modern evolutionary biology or physical cosmology. The writer noticed that some scientific findings and theories, like the anthropic principle, can actually be read as strengthening the position of theism (Lem, 1989)[12]. We can observe this change of attitude in his fiction: the 1971 short story *The Twenty-First Voyage*, my main point of interest in the third part of this paper, or the 1986 novel *Fiasco* present religious protagonists, monks and Catholic priests, whose theoretical positions are clearly supported by the writer.

Moreover, despite remaining an atheist for the reason pointed out above, Lem came to believe that a non-theistic image of the universe seems metaphysically deficient even to himself. He admits in the interview recorded in the beginning of the 1980s that "although I cannot agree to any form of a personal creator…and deny whatever gave rise to the world any personal properties, I also notice non-accidentality or explanatory insufficiency in the act of postulating total randomness of the rise of life and so humankind. There is a huge hole here in my ontology and my thinking which I cannot fill with anything. Anything!" (Bereś & Lem, 1987, p. 297)[13]. Interestingly, this confession is immediately caveated as he goes on saying that "in ten, fifty, or five hundred years, this dilemma may turn out apparent" (*ibidem*) because the sense of the metaphysical insufficiency may vanish in light of new scientific data or simply with a new *Zeitgeist*. So,

---

12. However, as Lem comments, due to the reasons presented in the previous paragraph of the main text, this would be a theism with a negative sign: "as viewed that way the universe seems to be a grim space joke made by some sort of a fiend" (Lem, 1989, p. 9).
13. Although this is a 1980s' declaration, it is foreshadowed by Lem's several works of fiction, including, as we shall see in the second part of this paper, the famous 1961 novel *Solaris*.

he concludes that "nobody, including myself, can jump out of their skin, their moment of time, because the horizon of knowledge in which we are stuck is impassable" (*ibidem*).

To sum up, the ageing writer exchanged the Enlightenment-inspired optimistic (or at least facetious) Voltairean atheism of his youth for the somber view of the hostile universe that produces immeasurable amount of suffering and only a few drops of joy. Consequently, he became even more distanced from theism, although, his mind was haunted by the impression of metaphysical incompleteness of the atheistic worldview. Most likely, that nagging impression spurred him to conduct a series of literary experiments with the idea of deity. The results of those experiments will be discussed in the two following parts of the present paper.

Imperfect creator and the horizontal transcendence

The idea of an impaired god first appeared explicitly in *Solaris*, Lem's most popular novel published in 1961. The novel's main protagonist, Kelvin, explains it to Snow, one of the two other scientists living in the research station orbiting over the titled celestial body:

> *I'm not thinking of a god whose imperfection arises out of the candor of his human creators, but one whose imperfection represents his essential characteristic: a god limited in his omniscience and power, fallible, incapable of foreseeing the consequences of his acts, and creating things that lead to horror. He is a…sick god, whose ambitions exceed his powers and who does not realize it at first. A god who has created clocks, but not the time they measure.*

He has created systems or mechanisms that served specific ends but have now overstepped and betrayed them. And he has created eternity, which was to have measured his power, and which measures his unending defeat.…This god has no existence outside of matter. He would like to free himself from matter, but he cannot…(Lem, 2016a, p. 206).

During the discussion that follows Kelvin denies that he describes the Ocean, the intelligent creature covering the surface of the planet whose supposed attempts to communicate with the crew of the station have caused them immense suffering. Nonetheless, their unfortunate predicament can be interpreted as a metaphor of the situation of human beings confronted with hostile and incomprehensible world. And when they eventually begin to understand the world, they realise that no malicious intention stays behind their calamities. However, the other possible option is, as Lem seems to suggest, that some intention is actually there, moreover, a good one, only not powerful enough to have the full control over the consequences of its own actions. The ocean that is apparently almost omnipotent in its region of the universe does not want to destroy the people or make them suffer. It most likely does not understand human idea of psychological harm and even if it does, it has no idea that someone would rather commit suicide than live with an incarnation of their most hidden and suppressed fantasies.

The concept of the imperfect creator is a recurring theme in Lem's prose. Its grotesque incarnation is presented by the two 1971 short stories *The Eighteenth Voyage* and

The Twentieth Voyage that belong to the collection *The Star Diaries*. In fact, they are variations on the same idea: they both put their narrator Ijon Tichy in god's shoes with the former getting him retroactively create the whole universe from one meticulously designed particle and the latter letting him manage the project of total amelioration of the history of the universe and the humankind by time travels. Obviously, both endeavours derail spectacularly. The cause of Tichy's fiasco is his gullibility: he trusts his staff too much and they let him down due to ambition paired with incompetence and stupidity. Or rather, this is what he tells us to evade full responsibility for the two colossal disasters. Either way, we have a picture of high-reaching good intentions, almost divine creative potential, but insufficient foreknowledge, and imperfect execution.

We can point to the other two Lem's stories that deal with the idea of imperfect creator in much more serious way. In his 1968 novel *His Master's Voice* (Lem, 2020b) it is suggested that a highly advanced space civilisation that developed during the previous cycle of the universe pulsating from one big bang to another was able to introduce into the structure of the next, that is, our cycle a signal that favours the emergence of life and encodes some kind of information. The signal's beneficial influence is rather scant: it prevents neither the Holocaust of biological evolution nor all the atrocities done by humans. However, an attempt to make a potentially lethal use of a phenomenon discovered thanks to a small piece of the signal people were able to read is thwarted by the very nature of the phenomenon: apparently, the sender deliberately introduced that mechanism to prevent self-destruction of less advanced civilisations, like ours.

The other example is an apocrypha included in the aforementioned 1971 collection *A Perfect Vacuum* called *The New Cosmogony* (Lem, 1983, pp. 197–229). It is a fictitious oration of a Nobel Prize laureate who develops a groundbreaking cosmological theory based on the assumption that the observed universe is a product of the game, a large-scale space engineering done by joint efforts of several highly advanced cosmic civilisations, the players. The transformation of the universe undertaken by those civilisations is not all about producing and destroying stars or galaxies but more about changing constants and basic laws of physics. The theory assumes that the goal of the whole process is to make the universe more friendly to new civilisations. Again, the influence of the players, despite their almost divine potential, is limited: they cannot (or do not want to) prevent the cruelty of biological evolution, internal wars, and self-annihilation of some civilisations. All that they achieve is to keep the civilisations away from each other by imposing the limit of speed at which information, energy, or matter can move across the universe (that limit is indeed very low as compared to space distances).

The two examples of imperfect creators depicted (or rather presupposed) in *His Master's Voice* and *The New Cosmogony* clearly share benevolent intentions. Contrary to Kelvin's description, they are rather aware[14]; but they are constrained by the fact that they have no existence outside of matter, therefore, some initial conditions are simply given to

---

14. The scenario in which a civilisation does not refrain from an attempt to make an inter-planetary contact is depicted in the last and one of the most depressing Lem's novel, the 1986 *Fiasco*.

them; they also must respect some kind of meta-laws of the universe, for instance, the laws of logic.

Lem's gallery of imperfect creators cannot be complete without Trurl and Klapaucius, the two robotic protagonists of yet another collection of his grotesque short stories, *The Cyberiad*. The tone of the oldest tales in the collection written in the 1960s is light; the author experimented with the form of a folk tale by filling it with hard science fiction content full of robots, machines, interplanetary travels and space kingdoms. However, the pieces that were added in the 1970s are weighted with serious philosophical message and bitter conclusions.

Trurl and Klapaucius fit surprisingly well Kelvin's description of a sick god: their ambition and self-confidence clearly go beyond the limits of their creative faculties, they can build any measuring instrument but some of the parameters of reality they measure appear unchangeable, their mechanisms betray them and even seek their death. The last two pieces of *The Cyberiad* tell the stories of their failed attempts to create a perfect society and a perfect world[15]. The first of them, *In Hot Pursuit of Happiness*, focuses on Trurl's efforts to produce creatures that would be able to live in eternal harmony and happiness. His initial success, the Extatic Contemplator of Existence, "a machine whose consciousness, cathodes all aglow, embraced whatever came beneath its gaze, for there was nothing in the whole wide

---

15. Unfortunately, due to the fact that the stories in question were added to the collection after the publication of *The Cyberiad* in English, the English-speaking reader will not find them in the volume. However, the first of them, *In Hot Pursuit of Happiness*, has been published separately in the 1973 collection *Views from Another Shore* (Lem, 1999). The second, called *Powtórka* (*The Repeat*), has not been translated to English so far.

world that wouldn't give it pleasure" (Lem, 1999, pp. 6–7), turns out being so stupid to the effect that it cannot discriminate good from bad, let alone enter social relations. As it gets more intelligent, it becomes suspicious and anxious about its own condition. Trurl's further experiments with breeding miniature civilisations on laboratory slides teach him, among others, that a condition of a society, particularly, its ability to survive and its oppressiveness, does not depend on its members' propensity to good or evil. It goes without saying that none of the civilisations he produces eventually turns out harmonious, many of them are even more appalling than ours. The second tale, *Powtórka*, tells the story of a newly converted robot-king who, driven with the same goal to create a harmonious being, commissions Trurl and Klapaucius to produce a whole alternative universe. The two constructors experiment with time going both directions, a world without matter, even a multiverse. However, all in vain: they fail to produce a better world because the source of the problems appears to lie not in this or that physics but, as it is discovered by Trurl at the very end of the story, in logic: he delivers a formal proof that it is impossible to create a perfect world (Lem, 2015, p. 495).

All of the entities that can be subsumed to the class of Lem's imperfect creators, both presented in serious prose and grotesque fiction, share a common trait: they can be imagined as ethically and scientifically advanced (post-)humans. In other words, they are intelligible to us as reasonable intentional beings[16]. The condition of intelligibility was

---

16. This is, by the way, the reason why Kelvin says that the Ocean on Solaris does not fall under this category. The Ocean is someone whose actions make no sense, so it may be a space anchorite or a divine infant (Lem, 2016a, p. 207).

explicitly imposed on the divinity by Hans Jonas in his *Gottesbegriff nach Auschwitz* (*The Concept of God after Auschwitz*): he noticed that the Hebrew tradition as it tells us about the revelation and the divine laws is incompatible with the concept of *Deus absconditus*, God's incomprehensibility (Jonas, 2016, pp. 27–28). The philosopher has a point: if we could not understand God's reasons, we would have no ground to say that He is benevolent[17]. In other words, there must be an affinity between the creatures and their creator if we are to ascribe any value to the latter. Does not such an affinity exclude God's transcendence? Lem seems not to care about this problem: his imperfect deities are transcendent only in a horizontal sense, that is, in their being superior to present-day humans. They are not designed to be worshipped but rather followed: they mark the goal of our recurring self-transcendence.

The writer states this explicitly in his 1981 *Golem XIV*. The titled supercomputer, by the way, yet another example of Lem's material demigod, makes a prophecy about the future

---

17. Lem makes a similar point in his *Non Serviam*, yet another apocryphal review depicting a group of artificial persons who consider validity of Pascal Wager: the atheistic disputant, clearly the alter ego of the writer himself, argues that God's responsibility, understood in terms of universal (that is, also human) reason, cannot be dissolved by means of mystery (cf. Lem, 1985). No wonder that from Lem's perspective God as presented in *The Book of Job* is a monster: "I cannot read it not having a feeling that I am reading a story of God's cruelty that a believer can rename to the Mystery but I am not able to....Certainly, I do not wish for such a God, I do not want to have anything in common with him. Here, I do not put his existence in question, it is by no means an anti-existential argument against theodicy but I say in terms of human-to-human proceedings: this is ignominious! Here, I part with anybody who bows humbly to this monstrosity. Faced with such an act I fall dumb and mute and I cannot say anything more" (Bereś & Lem, 1987, p. 171).

of humankind: our destiny as a space civilisation is to make subsequent transgressions of natural limitations, "ascend to heavens" after him, gain divine powers and knowledge, and finally, perhaps, break out from the universe as such (cf. Lem, 1985, pp. 167–169, 223–225). All of this on condition that we do not destroy ourselves (which we will most likely do sooner or later).

Deus absconditus and the vertical transcendence

A reader interested in Lem's philosophy of God and religion should follow the writer's own suggestions (cf. Lem, 2013a, p. 37) and focus in the first place on one particular work: *The Twenty-First Voyage*, yet another short story added to *The Star Diaries* collection in 1971. Although, it tells about Ijon Tichy's visit to a distant planet called Dichotica, we can easily notice that the narrator's journey is not really in space but rather in time: the writer aims at giving a prognosis of our civilisational development for the next millennium. What interests him the most is the influence of emerging biotechnologies on the Catholic doctrine. The story is written in a grotesque manner, particularly as it comes to describe various bizarre corporeal human forms resulting from biotechnological revolutions, but not without serious or even somber tones, as is often the case with Lem's prose.

Although, some particular moments in the fictitious future history of Church dogmatics are humorous (e.g. the idea to establish the order of the Prognosticant Friars whose task is to predict the future evolution of the doctrine is obviously auto-ironic), general claims that follow from it are clearly made with full assertoric force[18]. The 3000AD

---

[18]. Most of them are reappearances of claims expressed in Lem's fourth great essay, the 1970's *Science Fiction and Futurology*.

Church finally recognises historical volatility of the deposit of faith and the lack of its unalterable core. The magisterium comes to what Lem calls elsewhere the generalised Job principle, according to which: "nothing what happens *here* cannot be adequate to what is *there*" (Lem, 2009c, p. 181). As we shall see, the principle, together with its two other variants: epistemic (we cannot know what is *there*) and ethical (no actions here have consequences *there*), serves as a peculiar form of theodicy that makes Christianity extremely apophatic (cf. Szpakowska, 1996, pp. 42–43).

What can be the substance of faith that follows from such a principle and what can it mean to the believers? According to the short story, the fourth millenium Church comprises only old and useless generations of robots and computers. Those outdated artificial intelligences gather in monasteries or live the life of a hermit, but they do not cultivate any rites nor do they conduct any missionary activities. Worshipping God has no sense and value for future electronic theologians because they perceive religious practices of any kind as based on a presumption of a form of relation to the Creator modelled on a trade arrangement: you give us life and salvation, we give you prayer and adoration. And that presumption is rejected because it collides with the generalised Job principle. From God's perspective it should be of no importance whether one is a believer – let alone a worshipper – or not: the idea that He prefers believers is yet another layer of His anthropomorphisation[19]. Moreover, a perspective of individual salvation together with a vision

---

19. This aspect of Lem's philosophy of God has been developed in *Non Serviam*: according to the writer, God who rewards those who have chosen faith in a state of uncertainty can be neither good nor just (Lem, 1983, pp. 188–189).

of afterlife reward or punishment cannot appeal to a 3000AD post-human (no matter if biological or electric) because the idea of indivisible and absolutely durable subject that serves as their necessary presumption has been obsolete by technological progress: minds can be split and merged, formed and reformed at will. Therefore, faith has no purposes and makes no promises. In the words of one of the robotic Demolitian Friars, Father Memnar:

It is – one might say – completely naked, this faith of ours, and completely defenceless. We entertain no hopes, make no demands, requests, we count on nothing, we only believe....If someone believes for certain reasons and on certain grounds, his faith loses its full sovereignty; that two and two are four I know right well and therefore need not have faith in it. But of God I know nothing, and therefore can only have faith. What does this faith give to me? By the ancient reckoning, not a blessed thing. No longer is it the anodyne for the dread of extinction, no longer the heavenly courtier lobbying for salvation and against damnation. It does not allay the mind, tormented by the contradictions of existence; it does not smooth out those edges; I tell you – it is worthless! Which means it serves no end. We cannot even declare that this is the reason we believe, because such faith reduces to absurdity: he who would speak thus is in effect claiming to know the difference – permanently – between the absurd and the not absurd, and has himself chosen the absurd because, according to him, that is the side on which God stands. We do not argue

> *thus. Our act of faith is neither supplicating nor thankful, neither humble nor defiant, it simply is, and there is nothing more that can be said about it (Lem, 2016b, pp. 233–235).*

However, despite the lack of rites, hopes, or any content, there is a way the faith of robotic monks can still reveal itself: in their restraint from utilising the available technology of conversion. This technology can provide the Church total supremacy in evangelisation while not being any form of coercion and not depriving people from their freedom. It only forces one "to look into the face of Enigma, and he who sees it thus shall nevermore be free of it" (Lem, 2016b, p. 267). The very act of restraint from using such a means of mass conversion makes the Church independent of technology[20].

What is particularly convoluted in the doctrine of robotic monks of the fourth millennium is their approach to the idea of Satan. This is strongly related with the highly ambiguous role of freedom in the system of future theology. Freedom, due to technological advancement, is deprived of any constraints and therefore ceases to be a value. Instead, it turns into an unbearable burden, the abyss. Both individual people and communities are degenerated and frustrated by the boundlessness of freedom. Nonetheless, the Church doctrine understands freedom as God's gift; in the end, that was Him who did not impose on humans any impassable limits, neither external nor internal: they can reshape their environment as well as their bodies and minds at will. At the same time, the doctrine acknowledges demonic character of

---

20. As Jerzy Jarzębski comments, this is their "heroic keeping watch at the only window open for the transcendence" (Jarzębski, 2003, p. 287).

freedom and considers Satan as its personification. Satan is the progress of science and technology because the progress serves freedom. Therefore, he is the most important part of the Divine Plan, the part that is also the most terrifying. Satan is what is the most incomprehensible in God from the perspective of believers. One of the Prognosticants, Father Darg, the computer-monk, spells it out to Tichy as follows:

Satan is the idea that God can be delimited, classified, isolated, separated by fractional distillation until He becomes that – and only that – which we are able to accept and need no longer defend ourselves against. An idea which is untenable inside history, because it leads inevitably to the conclusion that there is no knowledge but what derives from Satan, and that he will extend his influence until he has encompassed all that fosters knowledge, in toto (Lem, 2016b, p. p.242).

Lem's electronic theologians admit that avoiding Manichean vision according to which evil is part of divine essence was difficult and forced the Church to recognise historicity of Satan as the constantly changing projection of the most appalling and destructive features of the Creation. Hence, the demonicity is understood as mediated by the believers' epistemic perspective. As Father Darg sums up: "God is Mystery, while Satan represents the personal aggregate of the isolated constituents of that Mystery. For us there is no Satan outside history. This is the one thing, constant in him and personified, which proceeds from freedom" (Lem, 2016b, pp. 244–245).

The prognosis of Catholic doctrine proposed by Lem in *The Twenty-First Voyage* can only be read, according to his own opinion about science fiction's epistemic capabilities he expressed in *Science Fiction and Futurology*, as probing the future by considering some possible scenarios (cf. Lem, 2009b, p. 23). Nothing of all that is certain: neither the prediction of further developments of biological and AI technologies, nor the speculation about their cultural and dogmatic ramifications. However, the scenario can be evaluated from the philosophical perspective because of its basic presuppositions.

It seems that the weakest point of the whole vision is inconsistency in Lem's conception of religious faith. On the one hand, the story's final passages about technologies of conversion presuppose the view that the whole point of faith is to have some beliefs, that is, to assert some uncertain propositions (cf. Lem, 2016b, pp. 261–266). On the other hand, the propositional content of the faith of electronic monks is extremely scant. Their one and only irrefutable dogma is total uncertainty regarding to who God is. So, their whole faith boils down to just the two simple beliefs: "There is God" and "God is Mystery." The historical perspective would add more content, that is, information about the intellectual process that has led to such a doctrine. However, that additional content can only take a form of reported speech expressions about things the ancestors once believed but are nothing more than children's fables to the contemporary believers (cf. Lem, 2016b, p. 247). From this perspective Lem's view would be not far from the standpoint defended by Richard Braithwaite in 1950s who interpreted religious content as a tale we do not tell with assertion any more (cf. Braithwaite, 1956).

However, one can notice that the propositional reading

of faith is intertwined with a different view, according to which faith has some intrinsic autotelic value independent of its utility and even its propositional content. This is closely connected to the fact that *The Twenty-First Journey* exhibits a peculiar approach to transcendence that is unique in the whole Lem's prose. God of the robotic monks on Dichotica is not an imperfect creator. They do not know who He is, they cannot understand Him. His transcendence is radical, we can say, vertical, because nobody can imagine being Him. The generalised Job principle places Lem among the proponents of apophatic theology.

Paul Tillich in *The Courage to Be* writes about a feeling called the anxiety of meaninglessness and emptiness. According to the philosopher, this is one of the three basic forms of existential anxiety besides the anxiety of fate and death and the anxiety of guilt and condemnation (cf. Tillich, 2008, pp. 41–44). It seems that Lem considers the latter two forms of anxiety as historically accidental because the civilisation is theoretically able to provide means to combat fate, death, and perhaps even guilt[21]. However, futuristic visions of humankind overcoming its limitations not only leave the anxiety of meaninglessness in us intact but also make it worse.

The anxiety of meaninglessness shows a possibility of another eschatology that is unreachable for any form of imaginary technology. Lem's generalised Job principle with all its consequences make room for that kind of eschatology. The ineffability of the ultimate meaning is no news within the apophatic tradition. The hope of such a meaning does not

---

21. This can be done e.g. in a form of the so-called ethicsphere, that is, an intelligent and protective environment that disables any evil action, as presented in Lem's 1982 novel *Wizja lokalna*.

need to entail a promise to reveal its mystery on any stage of individual existence. This hope could be a "firm" content of religious faith. Both biological post-humans and artificial intelligences could unite in it because it can be a final blow to the feeling of meaninglessness that haunts all of them.

The reading presented above is similar to the interpretation given by Jerzy Jarzębski. However, Jarzębski reads *The Twenty-First Journey*'s faith as a form of mystical gnosticism (Jarzębski, 2003, p. 291). He says that robotic monks, like the supercomputer Golem XIV, try to get out of their ecological niche, that is, ultimately, our entire universe. They all aim at transgression "into a cosmos of higher grade that stays above, dictates its own terms, and thus gives meaning to their world" (*ibidem*, p. 295). It is of a lesser importance to them if they meet God in that world. According to Jarzębski, "what is important is the dramatic postulate of the existence of an umbilical cord that connects our cosmos to the others as well as a phenomenon of multi-level…evolution that would bring the beings who inhabit our cosmos to a foothold of a bridge thrown between it and some other cosmos that would provide us with a cure of our existential anxiety" (*ibidem*).

I cannot agree to that reading because I believe that Jarzębski mixes the two different kinds of transcendence that should be set apart. Going beyond our cosmos, breaking out to the other, higher cosmos, as I pointed out at the end of the previous part of this paper, would rather be a form of horizontal transcendence. For if we speak about a reality outside as a "higher cosmos" connected to ours by a bridge that can be crossed one day, then that external reality is no longer totally separated and becomes conceptually tame as a field of a possible expansion: a moment we enter it will begin a process of its conquest and thus we will repeat the history of the conquest of our cosmos. This, again, will take meaning away from our existence and bring us back in a state of anxiety.

I also believe that the vision Lem presented in *The Twenty-First Voyage* is by no means gnostic. Dichotican electric monks believe in the vertical transcendence because their faith is based on the generalised Job principle that thwarts any access, even merely conceptual, to the other side. Their God is not an inhabitant of any super-universe, He cannot be approached, understood, let alone conquered. But can they say that their God is good? Does not the vertical transcendence exclude this predicate too? Not necessarily. Lem's visions reverse the aforementioned Western metaphysical tradition: the whole being is penetrated by evil, every action, no matter how benevolently intended, seems to bring disastrous effects. So, if we reverse definitions of good and evil accordingly, we come to the conclusion that good is a lack of evilness, that is, a lack of being and action. Therefore, the only way to be good is to be absent. Dichotican *Deus absconditus* satisfies that condition thanks to the generalised Job principle[22].

Concluding remarks

As it is argued in the first part of the paper, Lem's initial Enlightenment-style atheism transformed into a bitter fatalist vision of the evil-permeated universe that undermines

---

22. This part of the present paper is a developed version of the third part of my 2016 paper *Futurologia chrześcijaństwa według Stanisława Lema: Rozważania wokół «Podróży dwudziestej pierwszej»* (Gomułka, 2016, pp. 205–212).

any form of theodicy. However, while sticking to that later form of unbelief he was constantly nagged by a sense of metaphysical insufficiency. That sense prompted the writer to experiment with various deities capable of creating, or at least reshaping, the universe at will. The second part of the paper presents a gallery of Lem's demigods designed in accordance with Hans Jonas' guidelines for the idea of God after Holocaust. I attribute the concept of horizontal transcendence to that class of deities because, since they are understandable to us, they can serve as our role models that mark the direction of the process of our successive technological transgressions. The third part discusses an exception to this tendency that can be found in *The Twenty-First Journey*: a vision of a totally incomprehensible Absolute being a result of a thousand-year process of purification and refinement of Catholic doctrine. The vision is governed by the apophatic rule called the generalised Job principle and can be seen as an answer to our anxiety of meaninglessness analysed by Paul Tillich in *The Courage to Be*.

Now, we should consider yet another question that can arise during discussing Lem's approach to faith as presented in *The Twenty-First Voyage*: since his own nagging sense of insufficiency of atheism can be read in light of Tillich's anxiety of meaninglessness and since the doctrine of 3000AD electronic Catholics seems tenable, why does Lem remain an atheist for the rest of his life? The answer, I believe, lies in one fact that was omitted as we discussed the benevolence of *Deus absconditus*: the fact that theism entails a belief that the world has been created. Clearly, for Dichoticans, the incomprehensible God is nevertheless the Creator who set up all the rules, including those which they perceive as unbearable. True, as long as God does not act, He can be called benevolent. But the creation of the universe was an action, God was there, He had his fingers in it. The act of creation is a huge breach of the generalised Job principle. Now, we can ask Him a question, why does this world look as it does, a question that begs a theodicy. We can provide any divine exculpation as we like but we always end up in one of the two horns of the old dilemma: either God is non-benevolent (when the world looks exactly as He wanted it to be), or is He non-almighty (when He wanted something else but failed). A possible third way out of this would require to abandon our moral categories of good and evil – and this is perhaps the next big revolution that awaits Dichotican electronic theologians as they already stay at its doorstep with their embroiled concept of Satan – but this is not a solution Lem was ready to accept. Even if his works do open a possibility of a new post-humanist ethics[23], the author of *Solaris*, as an individual human being, did not decide to go beyond the horizon of humanist moral narrative.

Works Cited

Bereś, S., & Lem, S. (1987). *Rozmowy ze Stanisławem Lemem*. Wydawnictwo Literackie.

Braithwaite, R. (1956). An Empiricist's View of the Nature of Religious Belief. *Les Etudes Philosophiques*, *11*(3), 488–489.

de Warren, N. (2015). Torture and Trust in the World. A Phenomenological Essay. *Phänomenologische Forschungen*, 83–99.

Gajewska, A. (2021). *Stanisław Lem. Wypędzony z Wysokiego Zamku*. Wydawnictwo Literackie.

---

23. An insightful account of that aspect of Lem's legacy was given by Elana Gomel (Gomel, 2014, pp. 187–210).

Gomel, E. (2014). *Science Fiction, Alien Encounters, and the Ethics of Posthumanism: Beyond the Golden Rule*. Palgrave Macmillan.

Gomułka, J. (2016). Futurologia chrześcijaństwa według Stanisława Lema: Rozważania wokół Podróży dwudziestej pierwszej. *Ethos*, *29*(3 (115)), 198–213. https://doi.org/10.12887/29-2016-3-115-12

Jarzębski, J. (2003). *Wszechświat Lema*. Wydawnictwo Literackie.

Jonas, H. (2016). *Der Gottesbegriff nach Auschwitz. Eine jüdische Stimme*. Suhrkamp.

Kandel, M. (2016). Translator's Note. In S. Lem, *The Star Diaries* (pp. 337–338). Penguin Books.

Lem, S. (1983). *A Perfect Vacuum* (M. Kandel, Trans.). Harvest/HBJ.

Lem, S. (1985). *Imaginary magnitude* (M. E. Heine, Trans.). Harvest/HBJ.

Lem, S. (1989). Zasada antropiczna. *Wiedza i Życie*, *5*, 6–9.

Lem, S. (1991). *One Human Minute* (C. S. Leach, Trans.). Mandarin.

Lem, S. (1999). In Hot Pursuit of Happiness. In F. Rottensteiner (Ed.), & M. Kandel (Trans.), *View from Another Shore* (II, pp. 1–41). Liverpool University Press.

Lem, S. (2000). *Świat na krawędzi. Ze Stanisławem Lemem rozmawia Tomasz Fiałkowski*. Wydawnictwo Literackie.

Lem, S. (2008). *Dzienniki gwiazdowe*. Agora.

Lem, S. (2009a). *Biblioteka XXI wieku. Golem XIV*. Agora.

Lem, S. (2009b). *Fantastyka i futurologia: T. 1* (Vol. 1). Agora.

Lem, S. (2009c). *Fantastyka i futurologia: T. 2* (Vol. 2). Agora.

Lem, S. (2013a). *Sława i Fortuna. Listy do Michaela Kandla 1972–1987*. Wydawnictwo Literackie.

Lem, S. (2013b). *Summa Technologiae* (J. Zylinska, Trans.). University of Minnesota Press.

Lem, S. (2015). *Cyberiada*. Wydawnictwo Literackie.

Lem, S. (2016a). *Solaris* (J. Kilmartin & S. Cox, Trans.). Faber & Faber.

Lem, S. (2016b). *The Star Diaries* (M. Kandel, Trans.). Penguin Books.

Lem, S. (2020a). *Highcastle: A Remembrance* (M. Kandel, Trans.). MIT Press.

Lem, S. (2020b). *His Master's Voice* (M. Kandel, Trans.). MIT Press.

Lem, S., & Targosz, K. (2001). Wbrew nadziei mam nadzieję. *Przekrój*, 18–23.

Orliński, W. (2017). *Lem: Życie nie z tej ziemi*. Wydawnictwo

Czarne/Agora.

Płaza, M. (2006). *O poznaniu w twórczości Stanisława Lema*. Wydawnictwo Uniwersytetu Wrocławskiego.

Szpakowska, M. (1996). *Dyskusje ze Stanisławem Lemem*. Open.

Tillich, P. (2008). *The Courage to Be*. Yale University Press.

Masters' Silence. Lem's 'Alienomorphic' Model of Communication

Jarosław Boruszewski

Wrapped in a network of bugs and taps, we were supposed to establish contact with an intelligence that inhabited the Cosmos. — "His Master's Voice"

Introduction

"New Cosmogony" by Stanisław Lem – the final part of a collection "Perfect Vacuum" – is a text which cannot be genologically captured. It stands out from the collection itself, which is primarily a second-degree fiction, a collection of reviews of books which do not exist. It is an account of a lecture on a non-existent theory, admittedly with a non-existent book in the background, but this is just a pretext – a sort of kickoff for the topic. A presentation on the theory turns into a lecture on this very theory. The existence or non-existence of a theory is different from the existence or non-existence of books, but nevertheless this is not the subject of discussion here. New Cosmogony (NECO – the theory itself and not a fictitious book with such a title) is meant to solve Fermi's paradox, and it offers a possible solution of this paradox. However, this is still not the direct subject matter of the following paper[1]. NECO is not only cosmogony and cosmology, but also a complete vision of communication on a cosmic scale – "the idea of the palimpsest Cosmos-Game with its unseen Players who are perpetually alien to

---

1. Look for further information in Ćirković 2018.

one another" (Lem 1979: 200). In fact, within NECO *communication precedes cosmology*, and the physics of Universe is a result its sociology. However, this is not about traditional views of communication because their range is local. In the cosmic scale, the principles of communication are turned upside down, and this issue is mostly the subject matter of the following essay.

Lem outlined the main idea of NECO in his essay "Metafantasia: The Possibilities of Science Fiction" which was originally the end of a vast collection entitled "Fantasy and Futurology". In his essay, Lem presented three possible variants of the creation of SF: beginning with the classic game with the Nature through an idea developed in "Sexplosion" which could have a form of a hypothesis about the human nature and NECO as the final variant. Lem pointed out that NECO has a different creational potential from the remaining variants, and it cannot be captured within the known canons of fiction, because it is *a chronicle of an adventure of a certain idea* and not of some life adventures of chosen characters. In this respect, such a fantastic creation

> *would lead to a fractured work, with literary fragments, on the one hand, and discursive passages summarizing the new cosmogonic views, on the other. What is needed is an entirely new narrative structure, [...] perhaps a collage of excerpts from scientific texts, press clippings, the addresses of Nobel laureates, or other facsimiles.* (Lem 1981: 58)

This confirms the genological elusiveness of Lem's text with its conscious and intentional character. As I will show further, "Metafantasia" is not the only preview of NECO, and it also reaches back to Lem's early essays form the 1950s[2]. More importantly, one can see that the theoretical subversion of NECO is the aftermath of the dispute at the meeting of the Science Council from the last part of "His Master's Voice" (which is abbreviated as MAVO in the rest of this essay). To show this in more detail, the essay will be supplemented with a short narrative passage.

Before this is done, it is necessary to present an initial view of a metafantastic model of communication, i.e. a palimpsest of games carried out between distant cosmic civilizations. The great distances separating those civilizations make traditional communication impossible. One cannot send messages via physical signals. Even if this were possible, this would still be pointless as the content of signal after covering a huge distance would be out of date. However, this does not mean that communication is impossible:

they do not communicate with each other directly. They only infer the existence of their neighbors from certain observed facts: from certain gradual, noticeable changes in the laws of nature. […] communication in the universe occurs on the level of action, not in articulated messages. The civilizations do not fight, since it would do them no good, nor do they converse, since that would be meaningless. (Lem 1981: 56)

It is easy to see that this is the abandonment of the traditional view of communication and especially as far as its use in cosmic communication is concerned. In the use of

---

2. These are the essays collected in Lem's first non-fiction book called "Entry into Orbit" („Wejście na orbitę").

the classical concept, there is a sequence of solving particular alternatives: signal or non-signal, meaningful or meaningless, used for communication or not, meaning either known or unknown (Głaz 2014: 364). In NECO, everything is straightforward: if there is a signal, then it is meaningless. Such a statement taken literally *prima facie* seems to be a semiotic aberration. In order to outline its sense in more detail and expand the remaining alternatives, it is necessary to present the relation between NECO and MAVO first narratively and then analytically.

Narrative

The founder of NECO is Arystydes Acheropoulos, a renegade researcher, possibly a maniac or a genius who created on his own in isolation. He published a book called "New Cosmogony" which for a while was an object of interest for some historians of science and especially the ones fond of scientific eccentricity or even the pathology of knowledge. However, after some time Acheropoulos had a follower named Alfred Testa, from whom we learn the most about NECO. In his Nobel Prize speech, Testa pointed out that Acheropoulos had no predecessors. Due to Testa's success, specialists in para- or pseudoscience were no longer the only ones to know something about NECO. Research on the genealogy of the project of New Cosmogony began.

It was established that Acheropoulos was familiar with the publications on MAVO, and the objects of his in-depth research were primarily materials from the meetings of Science Council, where a confrontation of MAVO representatives with their adversaries took place. It was this episode which turned out to be crucial for NECO. The clash between the Project and the Alter-Project was the source for

Acheropoulos's postulates in his seditious theory. Therefore, let us remind ourselves some fragments from the materials from the meetings of Science Council which constitute the genealogy of NECO.

> *Two lectures of the representatives of the Alter-Project (Lerner, Sylvester) and two long speeches of the representatives of the Project (Hogarth, Rappaport) were given during the meeting of Science Council. Lerner's lecture was the inauguration of the meeting. He gave a detailed representation of his cosmogonic theory of the pulsating Universe which is a theoretical framework to justify the conclusion that one cannot talk about a message from the stars. According to the theory of the pulsating Universe, the alleged neutrino letter from the stars is a fully natural phenomenon and is an echo of the neutrino wave which made our Cosmos. Lerner's theory was thought as an elimination of the problem of the letter, and in this respect Lerner is quite straightforward:*
>
> *Nothing was sent to us by "neutrino telegraph" from another civilization; at the other "end" there is No One, and no transmitter, nothing but the cosmic pulse*
>
> *It is only an emission produced by processes that are purely physical, natural, and totally uninhabited, therefore devoid of any linguistic character, of content, of meaning...* (Lem 2020: 235)

The lecture was followed up by a stormy discussion with Hogarth's reaction as an important voice. He observed that Lerner turned everything upside down because he changed the whole Universe to adjust it to the letter. Lerner's chosen parameters "would correspond to the *given* energetics of the signal" (Lem 2020: 239, emphasis in original). Interestingly, Lerner smiled and said Hogarth was right although to some extent.

The next lecture was given by an astrobiologist Sylvester, who continued Lerner's theme of the pulsating Universe, but he also introduced into the discussion the thread of civilizations which emerge and perish to the rhythm of cosmic pulsation. Ancient high-tech civilization capable of foreseeing its forthcoming end wanted to influence the fate of the cosmos. With the help of astroengineering manipulation the civilization wants to send a 'biophilic' signal into the next cosmic phases. Such a point of view presupposes the existence of the authors of the signal who have already been dead for millions of years. The received signal which became the subject of the research of the Project is not a letter, but a causal impulse meant to 'adjust' the matter to the development of life. Sylvester's lecture was rich in highbrow comparisons and metaphors. However, it was Hogarth who organized Sylvester's hypotheses analytically:

> *The "signal" was no letter at all; its "life-giving"*
> *virtue did not represent one "aspect" as opposed to the*
> *"content." It was only that we, according to our*
> *custom, had sought to separate what could not be*
> *separated. […] We had failed to read it because for*
> *us, with our knowledge, with our physics and*
> *chemistry, to read it completely was impossible. […] it*
> *was addressed to the Universe and not to any beings.*
> (Lem 2020: 242-243)

Sylvester's theory resonated among the audience of the Scientific Council to some extent. However, in Hogarth's opinion, adjusting the whole Universe to a particular signal was a redundant conduct and possibly a breach of the principle of the economy of thinking:

it sufficed to admit, for example, that our receiving apparatus was primitive in the sense that a radio of low selectivity was primitive. [...] Perhaps the so-called letter was a recording of several emissions at once. If one assumed that in the Galaxy automatic transmitters were operating on precisely that "frequency", in that band, which we were treating as a single channel of communication, then even the constant repetition of the signals could be explained.
(Lem 2020: 244)

Rappaport was the last one to speak and he approached the same problem from a different angle, as in his opinion the semantic questions were more important than the technological ones. The differences in the development of the knowledge between civilizations are not only technological, but they also have a form of unassailable semantic limitations set upon the possible communication between the civilizations:

If civilizations spoke to one another in different languages, and their differences in development were considerable, at best those who were less knowledgeable would extract from the received communication only (or nearly only) what was physical in it (or natural, the same thing). They would

> *understand nothing more. And in fact, with a sufficiently large gap between civilizations, the same concept-symbols, even if they functioned in both cultures, would have totally different referents.* (Lem 2020: 248)

This exchange of theories and hypotheses proved crucial for NECO – the exchange itself, so not only the content of utterances but also their order and possible groupings. The exchange is initiated by the Alter-Project in its purely physicalist 'hard' variety, and this is continued by the Alter-Project but this time the variety is softer and presented from the perspective of life sciences. The project counters first in a 'hard' way relating to the technology of the detection of the signal and then proceeds to the 'soft' version concerning the communicative and semantic problems. Such an initial systematization of the discussion had to draw attention to the fact that NECO had to be comprehensive and tackle the subject multilaterally if not even aspire to versatility. And this became so, as Tiesta related. This is as far as the arrival point is concerned, but what about the starting point? It seems that if cosmogony is a game for everything, then one cannot appear humble and conservative. A firm blow is required, such as the one by the Alter-Project during the meeting of the Council. The universe has to be rearranged right away and in turn the consequences of this have to be drawn and more detailed problems and subtle questions discussed. This methodological brazenness gave NECO a momentum. To rearrange Universe according to…exactly what? As Hogarth observed and pointed out, the Alter-Project rearranged the Universe "to the *given* energetics of the signal" (Lem 2020: 239, emphasis in original), whereas NECO thought that what was given was *Silentium Universi* as "energetic silence" (Lem 1981: 57). The clash during the meeting of the Science Council which was the end of the MAVO Project provided NECO with omega and alpha (in such a sequence in the heuristic order). However, the creation of the New Cosmogony construct required some crucial supplements and detailed analyses.

Analysis

The findings from the meetings of the Science Council show that the problem of the Contact becomes stratified. It is obvious that there are two sides of the Contact. However, the problem on both sides breaks into at least three issues:

- authors, senders, transmitters;
- receivers, recipients, addressees.

The author is not necessarily the sender at the same time – the author is responsible for the content, whereas the job of the sender is to send the message. It is similar on the other side. The recipient is someone who actually receives the message, although this message does not have to be intentionally directed to the recipient by the sender. Consequently, the recipient is not identical with the addressee. Obviously, there are information and communication devices on both sides, transmitters and receivers. However, this is not only to complicate the matters or to find purely combinatorial possibilities. According to the Alter-Project, there were neither senders nor addressees. In Sylvester's view, there were at most the authors of the signal, but it was not directed to other civilizations, and subsequently, there were no addressees. As Hogarth points out concisely, according to Sylvester's hypothesis "our "code", though remaining an artifact, ceased to be a letter" (Lem 2020: 246). Sticking to the side of the senders only, one comes across a general trilemma: *a natural pulse, an artefact of an unknown civilization, a message*. The Project believed in the existence of the Senders. However, we were definitely not the addressees as these could be more advanced civilizations which "having passed a certain "knowledge threshold" were able both to detect the cleverly concealed signal and to decode its meaning" (Lem 2020:...). The problem with the Contact was placed by the Project on both sides of reception – *the imperfections of the receivers or the randomness of reception*. We accidentally find ourselves in the transmission not meant for us. What we can do is *to intercept what is physical in the message*. Therefore, the problems related to the Contact are of technological-instrumental and communicative-semantic nature. Within NECO, these problems have to be solved or they should not be allowed to emerge and should be eliminated.

There are still some elements missing in the foundations of NECO. Certainly, 'our' standard semantics has to be eliminated and there is no possibility to guarantee the compliance of the meaningful intention of the senders with the interpretation of the recipients. But one should also eliminate technological issues, especially the ones which are now reachable, and yet there is also no guarantee of the compliance of the standards of transmission and detection of the signal. So, what happens then? An essay called "The Technology of Miracle" written by Lem in 1954 may be helpful in this situation, where he mentions a very simple threefold model of technological development. Stage One is what we already know from the human history as a stage of primitive devices and faint theoretical knowledge. Stage Two involves parallel development and complication of both technology and scientific knowledge. As far as Stage Three is concerned, one encounters not only the breach of this parallelism but also *inverse of technological and theoretical complication*. With more theoretical maximization and complication comes minimalization and simplification of technological constructions. What is next?

> *Further growth of theoretical complication which will bring mechanical complication down to zero is not beyond thinking. We will then have a machine with no visible material parts (because its mechanical complication equals zero). […] In this way, by expanding in our minds the consequences of the law of technological development, we leave the real world behind and enter the world of philosophical paradoxes over which the theorists of cognition have been racking their brains since the ancient times. From this point of view, our considerations are not just child's play.* (Lem 2010: 169: own translation)

This essay contains a clue relating to the technological and instrumental aspect of the Contact. If the civilization of senders is more advanced than ours, then it does not use complicated transmitting devices and as such should apply non-material means of communication. On the other hand, according to Rappaport the less technologically advanced recipients are at most capable of understanding only what is physical. The problem seems to be turned upside down because in traditional communication studies a message is sent in the form of a physical signal carrying some sort of non-material content. However, the situation here is quite the opposite – *the message itself is non-material, whilst the content is physical*. How is this even possible?! One of the explanations could be carousel reasoning which to a great extent complicated the work of MAVO. This is not just only about the reversal of the relation between the premises and conclusions of reasoning, but also about switching the opposite poles in the encountered dualisms: "origin becomes telos, containment becomes emptiness, identity becomes difference, the spatial universe becomes a temporal moment, and information becomes mass and energy" (Csicsery-Ronay 1991:245-246). However, this is all about holding to one's position after taking a conscious ride on the carousel. In this situation, there is a *mutual change of the vehicle into the meaning, the medium into the message* and of the technological aspect of the Contact into a semantic one, and also the other way round. According to Lem's model of development from 1954 which became the missing element of NECO:

> *Instrumental technologies are required only [...] by a civilization still in the embryonic stage, like Earth's. A billion-year old civilization employs none. Its tools are what we call the Laws of Nature. Physics itself is the "machine" of such civilizations! And it is no "ready-made machine," nothing of the sort.*36 (Lem 1979: 208, emphasis in original)

Thus, there are both the authors of the message and its senders, but there are no technical transmitters or physical signals. Consequently, the letter from the stars does not exist or at least there is not one which makes us learn something about the laws of nature, e.g. such messages which are encoded formulations of the laws of nature. Obviously, the laws of nature are neither physical objects nor articulated messages. The fact that they use what we call 'the laws of nature' as tools for communication is undoubtedly peculiar and it is hard to grasp how a civilization which enters the Game makes the first move. All we know is that

They are silent, silent in keeping with their strategy […] they are making revisions, they are putting laws now moribund back into service. This is the reason they maintain their silence, which is a "strategic quiet." (Lem 1979: 219, 224)

So not only the manipulation of the laws, but also the accompanying silence – strategic quiet – constitutes the inter-cosmic communicative activity of the Players. This strategic quiet is the first component of *Silentium Universi*. There are two rules of SU within NECO, and the first one says that

no civilization of a lower order can find the Players, not only because they are silent, but also because their behavior in no way stands out against the cosmic background, and this because it is that very background. (Lem 1979: 221)[3]

The cosmic background is thus the second component of SU. It excludes random recipients, and there is no path for the transmission of the signal against the cosmic background

---

3. The use of the term 'behavior" in this translation is rather unfortunate. The original text in Polish contains the word 'postępowanie', which in this context would be better expressed as 'action' or 'conduct'. This is all about intentional activity of the Players aimed at a certain goal.

where 'younger' civilizations could find. But most importantly, *Silentium Universi* is at least analytically not a homogenous phenomenon – there is *the Silence and the Universe*, and more precisely silence against the background of universe. This is the key to understand how NECO solves the encountered problem:

> *The absence of signals from "Others," and in addition the lack of any trace of their "astroengineering feats," became a worrisome problem for science. […] They are nowhere to be found? It is only that we do not perceive them, because they are already everywhere. That is, not they, but the fruit of their labor.* (Lem 1979: 206-208, emphasis in original)

There is no signal, or the lack thereof, absence – nothing, *No Thing* – zero signal, a non-material message. There are no traces of activities of the Others and no trace is different from the rest because all the traces have been like this for quite a while. These are material contents of the inter-cosmic communication. This is the interpretation of *Silentium Universi* within NECO – *messages nowhere, contents everywhere* – "*everywhere*, literally" (Ćirković 2018: 134; emphasis in original). Carousel reasoning on a grand cosmic scale.

Discussion

The aim of this analysis was to show that NECO is a constructive response to many problems generated by the functioning of MAVO. However, I will not take the risk and say that this analysis solves or eliminates all the problems and I still have some doubts relating to the problems of ethical nature.[4] However, if you take into account the semiotic and communicative problems, it is hard to resist a statement that NECO begins where MAVO ends. This is clearly visible in the enclosure of the science within the encountered conceptualizations, an anthropomorphic understanding of communication and our cosmic conceptual solitude.[5] NECO is founded on a radically different, '*alienomorphic*' conceptualization of communication based on carousel reasoning and switching the vehicle and the content, as well as the medium and the message. In order to specify this conceptualizing maneuver, it is important to mention briefly the discussions which come from the literature on the semiotic problems of MAVO.

One of the problems of this kind is the question of the medium of communication and focusing on communication technology and not on the semantic problems. Anthony Enns suggested that the medium comes before the message, and that the failure to read the sense of the neutrino message was a result of the incapability to grasp it medium (Enns 2002: 37, 47). Undoubtedly, the second statement can be applied to MAVO, but it is hard to agree that the medium and not the message was in the foreground. Both points of view are equally important, and frequently the main problem was the question of the relation between the two point of view – whether they can be differentiated and if the material side is completely independent from the content or both sides are parallel[6]. If MAVO considered the medium to be precedent

---

4. Further information on the ethical questions generated by the lives and views of the representatives of MAVO can be found in: Rodnianskaia 1986 and Gomel 2014.
5. Malmgren 1993: 28-29; Głaz 2014: 369.
6. Part VIII of „His Master's Voice".

in relation to the message, then – after carousel reasoning – NECO would switch both sides, and yet this is not the case. The two components of *Silentium Universi* are equally important, both the strategic silence of the Players and the background of the Universe.

The next problem refers to the question from semantics and it was articulated by Istvan Csicsery-Ronay in his analysis of MAVO:

> *Unlike the silence of the universe, which like chaos can never be studied since it implies nothing, the neutrino message may mean a great deal. Indeed, it may mean everything, the very existence of the universe.* (Lem 1979: 218)

The above reinterpretation of the letter from the stars is a reversal of a direct conclusion from the failure of MAVO – the signal is meaningless. However, when it comes to NECO, such a reinterpretation cannot be defended because it is the silence which means everything. No single signal can mean everything. All the signals are meaningless – not only the neutrino letter, but also another ones. Only silence is meaningful.

Obviously NECO is not free from problems. There is one absolute canon of the cosmic Game which cannot be broken, and that is *Silentium Universi*. The Players "make themselves understood by methods that preclude the breaking of the rules of the Game" (Lem 1979: 218). However, it is known that only 'older' and advanced civilizations play this Game. The Players do not communicate with the younger civilizations because "they cannot specifically address such communications, and without an address they do not wish" (Lem 1979: 221). Therefore, the 'younger' civilizations are not the addressees in the cosmic communication, and they also cannot become random recipients. When do civilizations become the addressees? This is a mysterious matter – a sort of an aporia of NECO. When does the first stage of the Game, the classical game with the Nature end in order to become the second stage? This happens when the recipients observe certain anomalous changes. These anomalies can be quite spectacular and become, for example, eruptions or emissions of huge amounts of energy. In NECO, it is necessary to admit that the anomalies are not messages with a content, but they are a physical content of non-material messages. This can be understood in a situation of reception of cosmic communication. However, it is important to know that this is the content, and one needs to go beyond the current conceptual horizon: "Comprehension was arrived at gradually. These determinations, which undoubtedly did not take place all at the same time, opened up the next and second stage of the Game" (Lem 1979: 213). However, if random recipients are not the right addressees, as it was in the case of MAVO, then from the perspective of NECO another turn in carousel reasoning is made, and we stay in stage one of the Game, at the same time applying earthly semiotics to the 'letter of the stars', and we all know how this ends…

Works Cited

Csicsery-Ronay I., 1991, "Modeling the Chaosphere: Stanislaw Lem's Alien Communication", In N. K. Hayles Ed. *Chaos and Order: Complex Dynamics in Literature and Science*, Chicago, pp. 244-262.

Ćirković M.M., 2018, *The Great Silence. Science and Philosophy of Fermi's Paradox*, Oxford.

Enns A., 2002, "Mediality and Mourning in Stanislaw Lem's *Solaris* and *His Master's Voice*", *Science Fiction Studies* 29, pp. 34-52.

Głaz A., 2014, "Rorschach, We Have a Problem! The Linguistics of First Contact in Watts's *Blindsight* and Lem's *His Master's Voice*", *Science Fiction Studies* 41, pp. 364-391.

Gomel E., 2014, *Science Fiction, Alien Encounters, and the Ethics of Posthumanism. Beyond the Golden Rule*, Palgrave.

Lem S., 1979, *A Perfect Vacuum*, London, New York.

Lem S., 1981, "Metafantasia: The Possibilities of Science Fiction", *Science Fiction Studies* 8, pp. 54-71.

Lem S., 2010, *Wejście na Orbitę. Okamgnienie*, Warszawa.

Lem S., 2020, *His Master's Voice*, The MIT Press.

Malmgren C.D., 1993, "Self and Others in SF: Alien Encounters", *Science Fiction Studies* 20, pp. 15-33.

Rodnianskaia I., 1986, "Two Faces of Stanislaw Lem: On *His Master's Voice*", *Science Fiction Studies* 13, pp. 352-360.

Part 2.
Science as Fiction

Through a Mirror, Earthly: *Solaris*, Gaia, and the Search for Habitable Worlds

Emma Johanna Puranen

Solaris was published in 1961, the year that Yuri Gagarin became the first human to see our planet from outer space. Humanity was no longer bound to the ground – by the end of the 1960s, astronauts had looked back at our home from the surface of the moon. The new cosmic perspective, dubbed the Overview Effect, cultivated an understanding of the Earth as one whole system, not unlike the vast living ocean Kris Kelvin watches through the Solaris Station window (Yaden et al 1). Around the time *Solaris* was first translated into English in 1970, a chemist named James Lovelock was just beginning to publish papers on his newly-developed holistic theory of the Earth as a superorganism called Gaia, whose biosphere interacts with its environment in a self-regulating manner that perpetuates conditions comfortable for life. Lem's planet Solaris acts much like an intelligent version of Gaia, a planet-sized organism that regulates its orbit to maintain conditions for life. The same planetary imaginary that led to Gaia theory is reflected in Lem's portrayal of the intelligent alien consciousness of Solaris's ocean, as well as the futile attempts to understand it by the fictional science of solaristics. *Solaris* and Gaia theory both recognise the need to hold a mirror to Earth – "We don't need other worlds. We need mirrors" (*Solaris* 64), one character states. The text can also be read as a warning, displaying a unique understanding of the perils of anthropomorphism in humanity's attempts to understand nature, as well as of taking to space without first knowing the Earth – an understanding that I, as an interdisciplinary scholar working between astronomy and literature, apply to Gaia theory as well as the current search for habitable exoplanets. *Solaris* brings up a problem Lem saw in his contemporary world, one which can only be solved by a Gaian perspective that modern scientists have taken to heart. In this paper, I discuss Gaia theory not only in the context of modern science, but also in how it might have aided the solaricists.

A History of Gaia

Before it can be applied to *Solaris*, an explanation of the science of Gaia theory is in order. In the 1960s, James Lovelock worked at NASA's Jet Propulsion Laboratories as a consultant on the upcoming Viking missions to Mars. His team was tasked with designing an experiment to detect whether or not life was present on the red planet (*A New Look* 1-2). With Earth as his only example of life, Lovelock thought about how one could show that the Earth harbours life. He determined that one need only realise that the Earth's atmosphere is in a permanent state of disequilibrium. For example, it contains oxygen and methane simultaneously. These gases react and break down in sunlight, and are being constantly replenished by living organisms. Without this replenishment, the atmosphere would quickly return to an equilibrium state with greater amounts of carbon dioxide and water vapour. Earth's unlikely atmosphere is caused by the daily activity of its life. Therefore, Lovelock proposed that if the Martian atmosphere was also in a state of disequilibrium, that would be a major indication of a living world (*A New*

Look 5-7). The first paper to mention the concept of life altering Earth's atmosphere (though not yet by the name Gaia) was published in 1969 (Lovelock & Giffin), and in the 1970s Lovelock wrote *Gaia: A New Look at Life on Earth*, which would be the first of several popular science books on the topic. Thus, Lovelock's Earthly application of a problem designed for another world led to the original formulation of Gaia theory.

Scientific theories explain facts of the world, and as is the case for many theories, Gaia has been modified and supported over time with new data and observations. Gaia theory at first stated that the atmosphere is an extension of the biosphere – the sum of all lifeforms on Earth – and that the biosphere can be viewed as one entity that continuously alters the atmosphere for its own needs (*A New Look* 9). In the early 1970s, Lovelock further developed the theory with microbiologist Lynn Margulis, who stressed the importance of microorganisms within Gaia, as they were the sole life on Earth for the majority of the planet's history. She described Gaia succinctly as "symbiosis as seen from space" (Margulis 2). In addition to the case of the unlikely oxygen and methane detailed above, Gaia also provides explanations for other mysteries of Earth's climate history, like the fact that the sun has increased in temperature by 25% since life began several billion years ago, yet Earth's climate has remained stable over this time period. Gaia theory has life itself as the regulator (*The Vanishing Face* 108). It explains how Earth's biosphere contributes essential gases like oxygen to the atmosphere, and how these gases help maintain a hospitable temperature. As Gaia theory developed over the decades, Lovelock and his colleagues realised the original formulation was flawed in its sole focus on the biosphere, and came to substitute the whole Earth system (biosphere, atmosphere, oceans and surface rocks) for the biosphere alone, and to see the Earth as a superorganism (*The Vanishing Face* 112). "The evolution of the species and the evolution of their environment are tightly coupled together as a single and inseparable process" (*The Ages of Gaia* 11). That is, the whole Earth system, not life by itself, regulates habitability. Gaia comes from "interaction among organisms, the spherical planet on which they reside, and an energy source, the sun" (Margulis 119). Gaia theorists see the entire Earth as one entity, romantically named after a mythological goddess, that changes itself so it can remain a place where life can flourish.

Gaia theory was far from warmly received by the scientific community of the 1960s and 70s. Developed at the peak of the New Age movements and bearing the name of an Earth goddess, it was dismissed by many as a religious notion, or thought to be claiming that the Earth was an intelligent being (*The Vanishing Face* 106). Responding to this critique in 1990, Lovelock stated, "Nowhere in our writings do we express the idea that planetary self-regulation is purposeful, or involves foresight or planning by the biota" ("Hands Up" 100). Lovelock attributes much of the pushback against Gaia theory to effects of siloing of different scientific disciplines, as well as general discomfort with change. As described earlier, Gaia theory evolved with new scientific discoveries, and Lovelock welcomed that sort of critique, but felt his theory was disproportionately maligned. Lovelock believed boundaries between disciplines held science back, and Gaia theory reflects this in its core of interlocked systems

– it is not possible to understand Gaia from the vantage point of any discipline alone. "For Earth scientists their world was satisfying until Gaia loomed to falsify or complicate their elegant explanations. The same is true of field biologists; no wonder Gaia is unpopular." (*The Vanishing Face* 110) Other terms that have been used to describe Gaia theory include *biogeochemistry* and *Earth systems science*, both of which highlight the necessity of cross-disciplinary work to understand Gaia. The rise to prominence of fields like climate science, astrobiology, and exoplanet science have all contributed to Gaia's improved reputation. All three fields are fundamentally interdisciplinary and greatly enriched by the contributions of outside experts.

In grappling with the problem of how life might be detected, Lovelock dealt with a perennial challenge in the field of astrobiology (itself a field in its infancy during the Space Race), that is, the question of how to define life in the first place. Even today, scientists do not have one clear definition for life; different fields have different definitions, all of which capture some characteristics but none of which are fully satisfying. The autopoietic (referring to a system that can reproduce itself) definitions of life holds "an autopoietic system – the minimal living organization...[is] a network of processes of production (synthesis and destruction) of components such that these components: (i) continuously regenerate and realize the network that produces them, and (ii) constitute the system as a distinguishable unit in the domain in which they exist" (Varela 75). The Darwinian definition, used by NASA, says that life is "a self-sustained chemical system capable of undergoing Darwinian evolution" ("About Life Detection").

The autopoietic definition is non-concrete, and the Darwinian one suffers from its inability to account for animals that cannot reproduce, such as mules, and our lack of certainty about the universality of Darwinian evolution among life (Cortesão 4). Carl Sagan defined separate physiological, metabolic, biochemical, genetic, and thermodynamic definitions for life in 1970 (Sagan). While the attempts are valiant and each is useful, recounting them in full is not necessary to say that each definition again is lacking in some way, with biases towards certain characteristics and the priorities of certain scientific subjects (Cortesão 5-6). Indeed, the field of astrobiology suffers from a sort of Catch-22 in that it may well be impossible to define life until we find non-Earth-based life, yet without a definition for life, we may not be certain we can recognise such non-Earth-based life. The trouble comes from the simple fact that the only life we know of is from Earth, and it does not take a statistician to explain that drawing conclusions from a sample size of one leads to biased answers. Throughout this paper, I will refer to this challenge as "the sample size problem". It is fundamental to astrobiology and exoplanet science, and the need to weave together knowledge of many different fields to address it is the impetus for many current exciting interdisciplinary projects in those sciences. Lovelock, Lem's solaricists, and modern exoplanet scientists and astrobiologists all have their turns addressing the sample size problem.

A Living World: Solaris as Gaia, Gaia as Solaris

I argue that Lem's *Solaris* is a Gaian world – and the novel illustrates just how difficult it is for humans who crave categorisation to take on a Gaian view and understand such a world. The issue of the chronology of the formulation of

Lovelock's theory and the publication of Lem's novel will be addressed in a later section. In *Solaris*, humans are first attracted to the planet Solaris as an object of study due to its peculiar orbit. Solaris is in a binary star system, orbiting a blue sun and a red sun. This results in a complicated day/night cycle that Kelvin has trouble adjusting to, and a gravitational interplay between the two suns that makes it more difficult for the planet to maintain a stable orbit. Lem's fictional Gamov-Shapley hypothesis states that life is impossible on circumbinary exoplanets like Solaris, due to their elliptical orbits causing huge temperature fluctuations. Humanity notes with interest that Solaris – in spite of all physical characteristics of its system indicating it should be on an elliptical orbit and on a path to falling into its red sun – orbits in a circle, maintaining a constant distance from its suns (*Solaris* 16). Just as with Lovelock's life test and the tell-tale disequilibria in the Earth's atmosphere, it is a disequilibrium in Solaris's orbit that leads human scientists to discover that the planet is regulating its own environment to allow its life to prosper, in a very Gaian manner. It is fascinating to note that modern astronomers, in contrast with the fictional science portrayed by Lem, believe about 50-60% of circumbinary exoplanets can maintain stable circular orbits and thus could potentially harbour life, though this is still an active area of research (Jaime et al 260). On Solaris, just as in real science, a disequilibrium is a sign of life.

Lem's fictional science of solaristics fails to understand the planet Solaris and its sole inhabitant. Solaristics is a field plagued by uninterpretable data catalogues of the ocean's mimoids and rapidos and symmetriads, collapsing under the weight of theories that amount to little more than guesses.

Several chapters in *Solaris* consist of Kelvin recounting and pondering various (often contradictory) theories of solaristics. Early on, he explains that for a prolonged time period years before he was born, scientists hotly debated whether the ocean was alive at all, or whether it was merely a "gravitational jelly" abiotically controlling its orbit (*Solaris* 19). Biologists, physicists, and mathematicians all take turns attempting to define Solaris's ocean, which is given the scientific class *Metamorpha* (19). Solaricists attempt to catalogue the physical constructs that arise and collapse in the ocean, sending in instruments and trying to communicate with it by beaming x-rays into it (25). As the initial excitement of the discovery fades into confusion, public interest (and funding) for solaristics wanes. Solaristics is compared unfavourably to mediaeval scholasticism and called a "substitute for religion" (150), increasingly complicating itself, devolving into semantic arguments, and taking a long time to come to a consensus. The presentation of solaristics parodies some of the worst of science, such as the temptation to cling to antiquated disciplinary boundaries and experimental methods even when presented with a new object of study that clearly does not conform to these, the same tendency Lovelock called out in some critiques of Gaia. Solaricists do not only fail to communicate with the ocean of Solaris, they fail to communicate amongst themselves and with the public.

The debates in *Solaris* between scientists of different stripes are reminiscent of the differing definitions of life by scientific discipline. In the waning days of solaristics, Lovelock's *Vanishing Face* quote included earlier could easily be altered to fit into the text of *Solaris* as "For Earth scientists their world was satisfying until [Solaris] loomed to falsify or complicate their elegant explanations. The same is true of field biologists; no wonder [Solaris] is unpopular" (square brackets indicate substitution). Through Kelvin's historiographical recounting of solaristics, it reads as a field in urgent need of a more universal – Gaian – perspective. Solaristics never manages to become a unified field, but Lem's protagonist Kelvin – who, though ultimately unsuccessful, comes closer than anyone to communicating with the ocean in a very short time – is an able polymath, a psychologist who can operate medical equipment and perform neutrino physics calculations. However, for the human scientists attempting to replicate their field practices on Solaris, the leap is simply too large to manage. "A human being is capable of taking in very few things at one time; we see only what is happening in front of us, here and now. Visualizing a simultaneous multiplicity of processes, however they may be interconnected, however they may complement one another, is beyond us" (*Solaris* 103). Lem's contemporary science was lacking a planetary perspective, and not long after *Solaris* was written, Gaia theory came along, attempting to make the incomprehensibility of a planetary scale comprehensible. Could a Gaian perspective have aided the solaricists?

Solaris suggests that even the discovery of another world with life might not do very much to diminish the sample size problem. Statistically, in this case, two is not much better than one, and Lem's solaricists find themselves frequently comparing Solaris to Earth and its creatures. The ocean itself is constantly anthropomorphised in the text – "a hum so low and deep it seemed to be the voice of the planet itself" (*Solaris* 5), "foam the colour of bone" (10), "glinting bloodily" (11), "like a flexed muscle" (97), and "constant though extremely slow contractions of a muscular naked torso" (175) provide just a few examples. Kelvin is aware he is doing this, and is distraught by it, but bows to its necessity as a creature of the Earth himself with no other comparisons to reach for. In contemplating the structures the ocean builds, Kelvin describes "Seen from high up, a mimoid looks like a city; but this is an illusion arising from the need for any sort of analogy with something familiar" (98). The text is even more explicit when mentioning "the anthropomorphism and zoomorphism constantly present in the scientists' desperate quests" (100) and "a geocentrism that would be amusing if it weren't for his helplessness" (96). The effect is one of the solaricists grasping frantically for a missing piece, a feeling familiar to anyone who has tried to ponder the fundamental questions of astrobiology. Lem is hyperaware and critical of categorisation and the sample size problem in science, and he portrays both through solaristics.

I have thus far presented the ideas from *Solaris* without explicitly tying them to Lem. It is necessary at this point to take a step back and analyse the different approaches used by Lovelock and Lem in presenting their planetary superorganisms. *Solaris* is a novel. Though Lem states that he works hard to present plausible science in his novels ("An Interview", *Missouri Review* 231) – and I, as a scientist, find that much of what is presented in *Solaris* is plausible for Lem's time of writing – *Solaris* is still fiction. Lem, with his history of failing out of medical school by taking an idealistic stance of refusing to regurgitate the false scientific ideas that were approved by the Soviet authorities, turned to science fiction literature as a space in which he could publish more freely under the guise of fiction. Even there, his early works were held up for years by censors (222), and though he states that he is not concerned with how publishers or markets might see his work and instead writes whatever he wants ("An Interview", SFS 8), it is hard to believe safety was not a consideration in his move to sf. The constant concern of state censorship and the ever-changing list of ideas that were currently in favour – as well as living in a society that had fewer disciplinary boundaries than the West – no doubt contributed to Lem using science fiction to discuss ideas he might otherwise have written essays on and more clearly tied to his own name and opinion. A key example is his penchant for including imaginary literary reviews in his books, on display in *Solaris* with Kelvin's histories of solaristics. This provides a safety net for Lem, as "the succession of screens makes it impossible to tell which of the various personae, the imaginary author, the imaginary reviewer, or Lem, is really speaking" ("Interview", *Missouri Review* 219). The character of Kelvin provides an extra layer to *Solaris* in between the author and the reader that does not exist in Lovelock's popular science books about Gaia, in which Lovelock frequently writes in the first person and occasionally clearly interjects his own opinion. Lem and Lovelock were born just two years apart, and were both once medical students. That Lem portrays and critiques the fictional science of solaristics from the distance of a novel, whereas Lovelock critiques the real sciences of geology and biology for their rigid boundaries in scientific publications, speaks to the different socio-political environments in which they wrote. To determine how many of the ideas of *Solaris* are actually held by Lem, one must turn to Lem's interviews and non-fiction writings, which will be done later.

Solaristics is a field looking for its own version of Gaia theory, but *Solaris* as a book concludes that, for humans, extra-terrestrial worlds and extra-terrestrial life are fundamentally unknowable. Crucially, there is room for the unknowable in Gaia theory. It is possible to understand the big picture, the fact that the biota and the environment are interconnected and that ecosystems re-balance whenever one cycle nudges off-kilter, without knowing the minutiae of each cycle from the atomic to the oceanic scale. (In fact, the huge complexity of how these systems interweave and our lack of knowledge of that complexity is why humanity is a long way from being able to consciously tweak or alter Earth's ecosystems without fear of wreaking havoc.) For all that Kelvin recognises that the "guests", including Harey, are a form of communication from the ocean, he ultimately knows "she's basically a mirror reflecting part of [his] brain" (*Solaris* 134). Humans are individuals, the ocean is "devoid of such a concept" (90). Even in ruminating on the unknowability of the ocean, humans are projecting onto it. Some see Solaris as "a gigantic brain more advanced by millions of years than our own civilization, that it was some kind of 'cosmic yogi,' a sage, omniscience incarnate" (22). This description could easily be from a critic (or follower) of some of the more New Age interpretations of Gaia. Humanity looks to the planet Solaris for answers, but they find none, because they are looking in the wrong place. The source of all this frustration, this anthropomorphism, and this burning desire to understand Solaris's ocean is the need to understand Earth and humanity – it is the need to look into a mirror. Gaia theory as applied to Solaris might not immediately help the solaricists, but first applying it to Earth might.

Searching for Earth's Twin

Science has accomplished much in the days since we first took on a planetary perspective. *Solaris* was written over three decades before the first real-life discovery of an exoplanet – a planet outside our solar system. The truly alien nature of Lem's intelligent ocean world has held up better than most science fiction planets to the strange nature of real discovered exoplanets. The first exoplanet discovered orbiting a sun-like star was a gas giant similar in mass to Jupiter, but unlike Jupiter it orbited blisteringly close to its star. This "hot Jupiter" was found in 1995 ("What is an Exoplanet?"), and since then the catalogue of exoplanets has exploded, to the point where my naming a number would be futile, as it would surely change by the time of publication. Suffice it to say over four thousand worlds have been discovered, and this is barely scratching the surface (*NASA Exoplanet Archive*). In addition to hot Jupiters, we have found other classes of planet that do not exist in our own solar system, such as "Super-Earths", planets bigger than Earth but smaller than gas giants ("What is an Exoplanet?"). Solaris, "twenty percent larger than Earth in diameter" and "almost in its entirety covered by ocean" but for a "few plateaus" can anachronistically be called an oceanic Super-Earth – the term did not exist when Lem wrote (*Solaris* 16). Interestingly, it is thought that real oceanic Super-Earths are unlikely to sport islands on their surface as Solaris does, instead being entirely covered in oceans far deeper than any on Earth (Baxter 106). These oceans would reach depths at which water hardens into exotic forms of ice not due to temperature, but because of intense pressure (Léger et al.; D'Angelo and Bodenheimer). But in the time that Lem wrote *Solaris*, the mere existence of planets outside our solar system was not known for certain.

In all the thousands of exoplanets discovered, it is the handful believed to reside in their stars' habitable zones (the distance from their stars where the temperature on the surface could support liquid water) that draw the most interest. Media outlets eagerly report discoveries of the most Earth-like exoplanets to date, and scientists excitedly search for Earth twins. We are looking for another Earth – we are looking for Lem's mirror. This is in spite of the fact that it is easier to detect exoplanets that are more massive and orbit closer to their stars, and our planet-finding missions are consequently biased towards those ("What is an Exoplanet?"). Instead, astrobiologists "follow the water" to use NASA's long-time mantra, coined due to the necessity of water for all life on Earth. Harkening back to Lovelock in the 1960s, they look for atmospheric disequilibria and biosignatures. Exoplanet scientists are developing techniques to search for the chemical signatures of these biosignature gases – gases like methane and oxygen that are thought to indicate life – in the atmospheres of exoplanets. These "may be used to infer the presence of a gas or surface feature, which then may be interpreted as originating from a living process" (Schwieterman et al. 666).

It cannot be stressed enough how difficult these techniques are – scientists detect exoplanets by looking for minute wobbles in host stars that indicate the gravitational effects of a planet, or else looking for a slight dip in the light coming from a host star as the planet passes between it and Earth. Exoplanets are, with few exceptions, too dim and far away to directly image, since Earth receives very few photons of light from them. Yet, from very faint signals, scientists are able to use these impressive techniques to construct basic profiles of these far-off worlds ("What is an Exoplanet?"). More detailed atmospheric analyses, however, are not currently possible and will have to wait for upcoming missions. To give a sense of the timeline – in the mid-2020s the space telescope mission WFIRST might be able to detect biosignatures from planets orbiting nearby stars, but consistent exoplanet atmospheric characterisation may have to wait until missions of the calibre of LUVOIR, a concept being proposed for launch in the 2030s (Schwieterman et al, 695), or the European Space Agency's ARIEL, scheduled for launch in 2029 ("ARIEL"). For now, we wait. Despite the plethora of discovered worlds, our resources, telescopes, and funding are limited, so the sample size problem dictates that we look for what we know indicates a world that can harbour life.

If we cannot look to exoplanets for life just yet, the solar system is much more readily available. The recent case of the disputed discovery of phosphine on Venus provides an example of the difficulty of searching for biosignatures, and the difficulty humanity might have in recognising life even if we were to find it. When Lovelock was proposing his atmospheric disequilibrium method to search for life on Mars, we had yet to send missions to our neighbouring worlds. There were still those, inside and outside the scientific community, who harboured serious hopes of finding intelligent life on Mars or Venus. Although we have since found these worlds to be devoid of advanced life, the search for microbial life on both worlds is still ongoing. Venus was revealed to be an inhospitable pressure cooker of a planet with the first probes in the 1960s. However, high up in the cloud decks, there is thought to be an environment more amenable to life. Communities of microbes in the clouds of Venus have been theorised for decades (Morowitz and Sagan 1259).

In late 2020, Greaves et al published a paper in *Nature* announcing the discovery of phosphine in the atmosphere of Venus. Phosphine is considered a strong biosignature on rocky planets. On Earth, it is uniquely associated with biological origins, and phosphine should quickly be destroyed in the atmosphere of a rocky planet if it is not continuously replenished ("Phosphine Gas" 2). Greaves et al reported a detection of phosphine at an abundance of 20 parts-per-billion. The authors rigorously checked all known abiotic methods for creating phosphine – photochemistry, volcanoes, even meteoritic delivery – and determined that the phosphine originated either from an unknown abiotic pathway, or potentially a biotic one ("Phosphine Gas" 1). A month later, a different team led by Villanueva reanalysed the original data and published an article claiming Greaves et al had committed calibration errors and their claimed phosphine result was actually caused by sulphur dioxide (Villanueva et al. 3). This then led the original team to publish a re-analysis of their data maintaining that phosphine did exist in the Venusian cloud decks, albeit at lower levels than they had originally announced ("Re-Analysis" 1). This response was published near-simultaneously with a paper by yet another team, led by Snellen, that analysed the data from one of Greaves et al's sources (ALMA, the Atacama Large

Millimeter/submillimeter Array) and found no statistically significant detection of phosphine (Snellen et al. 1). An abundance in the range of parts-per-billion is far smaller than could be detected in an exoplanetary atmosphere given current technology, but this example still illustrates the difficulty and ambiguity in the search for biosignatures, even in our own backyard. I want to emphasise that no one on Greaves' team is claiming to have discovered life on Venus, merely a candidate biosignature – and yet, the flurry of response papers shows the strong interest the subject of biosignatures evokes.

I argue that *Solaris* portrays a convincing example of what a future discovery of extra-terrestrial life might look like – that is, confusion, struggles with definitions, and debates over whether or not the proposed life is actually life. The danger that this state of limbo presents to humanity is laid out on page 149: "The very existence of the thinking colossus would never let people abide in peace again. However much they travelled across the Galaxy and made contact with civilizations of other beings similar to us, Solaris would present a perpetual challenge to humankind." The initial excitement, continuous reanalyses, and eventual consternation of the solaricists occurs even with an entire alien planet and intelligence available to them. Our real-life situation is one in which far less information is available.

Is the search for life elsewhere in the universe then doomed to disappointment? Perhaps not – there are major differences between the situation of modern astrobiologists and that of the solaricists. A major pitfall of the solaricists harkens back to the sample size problem and the tendency to anthropomorphise. "Human beings set out to encounter other worlds, other civilizations, without having fully gotten to know their own hidden recesses, their blind alleys, well shafts, dark barricaded doors" (*Solaris* 136). The solaricists began studying an alien world without fully understanding their own. To paraphrase Snaut in the speech that contains the mirror quote, they saw themselves as looking to make contact, to share ideas, but in reality they were searching for other people, people in whom they could see their own futures or pasts (64). The ocean of Solaris provides that literally in the form of the "guests", constructed from the brains of the solaricists – the mirror they did not know they were looking for. Through the guests, the solaricists manage to have an interaction with an alien intelligence in which they learn absolutely nothing about the orbit-altering colloidal ocean outside the station windows, not even whether the creation of the constructs was a motivated or intentional act.

Solaris warns that ascribing a search for humanity – for a mirror – to an alien world is fundamentally futile if we have not yet held that mirror up to our own Earth. Earth is available to us – by venturing into space, we gain a new perspective on it, one that can spark ideas like Gaia – and though it is natural to look for life on worlds that have characteristics in common with Earth, we cannot truly find Earth in the cosmos when it is right beneath us. While scientists wait for the upcoming James Webb Space Telescope and other technological breakthroughs that will allow them to learn more about the atmospheres of exoplanets, they do what Lovelock did in the 1960s. They turn to Earth as an example, an analogue, getting to know its "hidden recesses". Lovelock looked to Earth as an example for Mars, and exoplanet scientists look to Earth as an example for exoplanets. I am using Earth as Gaia as a model for Solaris the living entity. We are all looking harder than ever at the Earth. Understanding our planet as a connected system, and, crucially, understanding humanity's role within that system, is essential to avoid the mistakes of the solaricists. Gaia theorists, and their descendants in the form of today's astrobiologists and exoplanet scientists, understand this.

Holding a Mirror Up to Lem

"We don't need other worlds. We need mirrors" (*Solaris* 64). Scholars and fans of science fiction frequently tout the genre's predictive ability. An oft-cited example is the case of the communicators from the original *Star Trek* series becoming reality in the form of flip phones. Listening to the mirrors quote, it would be more accurate to say the *Star Trek* writers were inspired by existing technology around them, and the engineers who designed flip phones were in turn inspired by memories of the *Star Trek* episodes they watched in their youths. The answer is more complicated yet less satisfying, to paraphrase Lem it is reflective, or as Le Guin famously put it "Science fiction is not predictive, it is descriptive" (xiv). N.K. Jemisin called science fiction "the aspirational drive of the Zeitgeist" (Hugo Awards 2018). Authors tap into the feelings of the time and write out *what-if* scenarios. If these scenarios occasionally come true, it is because the seed was already there. Science fiction, for all its alien vistas and strange biology and travels to distant galaxies, is always a commentary on the human condition and the writer's contemporary world. *Solaris* is no different, reflecting many of the hopes and fears Lem saw around him the early 1960s. Indeed, Lem saved his predictions for his philosophical work *Summa Technologiae*, rather than his fiction.

Was Lem aware of Gaia theory when he wrote *Solaris*? Chronologically, it would seem impossible, as *Solaris* was published in Polish in 1961 and Lovelock did not begin formulating Gaia theory until a few years later. Yet Lovelock himself admits that the beauty of Gaia lies in its simplicity, and that "the idea that the Earth is alive in a limited sense is probably as old as humankind" (*The Ages of Gaia* 9). It is no coincidence that the theory is named for the ancient Greek goddess of the Earth, and reading about it, it is easy to see the connections between ancient thoughts and modern knowledge. But even in the realm of science, Gaia theory was expressed before Lovelock. While Lovelock is hailed in the west as the discoverer of Gaia theory, the concept was well-known in the Russian-speaking world long before Lovelock began publishing. The Russian and Ukrainian mineralogist Vladimir Vernadsky, who played a large role in developing the idea of the biosphere, understood already in the early 1900s that the biosphere's evolution was inextricably interconnected with geological forces (*The Ages of Gaia* 9-10, *The Vanishing Face* 164).

Lem was certainly a prolific reader of scientific papers, both popular writing and journal articles – so much so that he was asked to write a future of the field of biology for the Polish Academy of Sciences ("An Interview", *SFS* 12). That Lem was well-versed in science is evidenced by his fictional Gamov-Shapley hypothesis, mentioned earlier, which in *Solaris* alerts humanity to the titular planet's strange orbit. Although most of the solaricists mentioned in the literature review chapters of *Solaris* are from the future and made-up, Lem's "Gamov-Shapley hypothesis" is named for real 20th-century scientists. It functions in the book as an older theory, previously thought rock-solid until disproved by the planet Solaris. George Gamow was a Ukranian physicist who defected to the United States (his name is given in Russian in the English translation of *Solaris*) and Harlow Shapley was an American astronomer. Though Shapley's "liquid water belt" idea planted the seeds for the concept of a star's habitable zone (Shapley), the distance at which liquid water could exist on a planetary surface, the idea that planets in the habitable zone might be unlikely around binary stars originated with Huang (Huang 106). Therefore, it seems Lem's "Gamov-Shapley hypothesis" came from his reading of contemporary science papers. Both Gamow and Shapley were popular science writers with interdisciplinary interests likely to be appreciated by Lem. "Gamov and Shapley expressed their interest in extradisciplinary questions such as the nature and origin of life with less devotion to the coherence of the sciences or their inherent oneness…Instead, they established ways in which the sciences could be fashioned into a whole that would suggest directions for future research and shape the meaning of what it meant not to know as much as to know" (Zakariya 436). A philosopher of science like Lem would surely be drawn to the unknowns of science, ideas which are explored in both Gaia theory and *Solaris*.

Lem's non-fiction writings provide evidence of his familiarity with Gaian ways of thinking, though his statements are contradictory and his exact view is characteristically hard to pin down. From his *Summa Technologiae*, published in Polish a year before Lovelock's first Gaia paper: "Biological evolution is not limited to this process since it builds higher entities — not islets anymore, but whole islands of homeostasis — from organisms, from phyla, classes, and plant and animal species. In this way, it shapes the surface and atmosphere of the planet" (25). Here he demonstrates Vernadsky's understanding of the interplay between the biotic and abiotic parts of the Earth, and how life alters its environment, key Gaiain principles. However, he contradicts this on the next page, saying "unlike most animals, man does not adjust to his surroundings", countering his earlier Gaian statement that the biosphere and its environment evolve together. This is very similar to a quote from *Solaris* that must be addressed. In describing the ocean of Solaris and its mastery of its orbit, Lem writes that "Put simply, unlike terrestrial organisms it did not adapt to its surroundings over the course of hundreds of millions of years, so as only then to produce a rational species, but it had gained control over its environment from the start." (18). This is counter to Gaia theory, which emphasises that organisms and their environment evolve together, and that intelligence is not necessary to alter one's habitat. Unlike the ocean of Solaris, Gaia is not intelligent, but instead acts unconsciously to affect its habitat. This statement is one of the few Lem makes directly about the Earth in *Solaris*, and it is made in the context of Kelvin recounting the history of solaricists, who, of course, moved to explore other worlds "without having fully gotten to know their own hidden recesses" (136). Solaris, however, is presented as a world where the biosphere is intertwined with the abiotic parts, a symbiotic superorganism that maintains the perfect conditions for its own prosperity by continuously affecting its orbit. It reaches homeostasis by causing a constant disequilibrium. Lem presents Solaris as a Gaian world, one explicitly seen as a mirror for Earth by the solaricists. It stands to reason the solaricists may have a changed view of the coupling of Earth's own biosphere and environment after their time on Solaris.

Lem speaks in his interviews of the unique importance of the Earth. "The only thing we have learned so far, and which fascinates me personally, is that the Earth is *the* heavenly body which by its lively blue colour differs dramatically from all other planets, and that seems like a tiny drop of life in this cosmic lifelessness" ("An Interview", SFS 9). Lem expresses concern over the militarisation of space (9), and, while they are not part of a military, his solaricist characters see themselves as "Knights of the Holy Contact" (*Solaris* 64), and travel to another world without fully understanding the Earth. Pak reads this "failure to accept earth by extending the boundaries of human identity to crowd otherness out" as "a psychological strategy of colonial imposition" (110). Unwilling to confront themselves and their own Earth, or understand the preciousness of their Earth, the solaricists journey to another world, where their folly is revealed by the ocean mirroring their thoughts and fears in the form of the "guests". When asked in an interview whether his fiction has something to teach, Lem responded "Yes, it has, but chiefly in teaching something about man, and not necessarily about unknown beings" ("An Interview", SFS 10). This, finally, is a paraphrase of the mirror quote from Lem himself, rather than filtered through Snaut or Kelvin or any other fictional character. Even amidst the excitement of the Space Race, Lem had the foresight to worry that humanity would make the mistake of forgoing the Earth, shunning the only place known to be human-habitable in favour of the cosmos.

Indeed, the most important lesson to be taken from *Solaris* is a Gaian one – that humans do not stand alone at the top of a hierarchy of Earthen life, but as one small part of a whole. This view is taken by Bruce Clarke in his description of a 1960s planetary imaginary that "renovates intuitions of the actual Earth in its complex operations or...inspires new fictive worlds to refract those processes for us" (151). He explores the worlds of Herbert's *Dune* and Gibson's *Neuromancer* through this lens, focusing not on the human, but on the planet-wide, ecological scale often considered too vast for comprehension and outside of human control (153). It is perhaps even more applicable to the literal planet-wide intelligence found in *Solaris*. The sheer magnitude of Solaris's ocean, as well as the magnitude of Lovelock's Gaia, both perform the duty of this planetary imaginary, in showcasing worlds as complex wholes. Kelvin's own journey as a solaricist concludes when he visits the old mimoid, sitting by the ocean and "playing" with it. "Staring in wonderment, I was descending to regions of inertia that might have seemed inaccessible, and in the gathering intensity of engrossment I was becoming one with this fluid unseeing colossus, as if — without the slightest effort, without words" (*Solaris* 177). Kelvin forgives the ocean and accepts its unknowability. This is exactly the method Lovelock recommends for learning about Gaia: "The simplest way to explore Gaia is on foot. How else can you expect to be part of its ambience? How else can you reach out and explore with all your senses?" (*The Ages of Gaia* 8).

Gaia theory is humbling, as Kelvin understands by the end of *Solaris*. As Clarke puts it, "This Gaian ethic is anything but escapist in its recognition that, no matter how high-orbital or cosmic we may go, we will remain systemically coupled to the ecological conditions of our own mundane and Earthbound situation" (190).

The irony in Lem's mirror quote is that Solaris is one of the least mirror-like science fiction worlds. Many science fiction worlds, forgoing the expectations of astronomy for convenience of storytelling and plot, are places where human characters can breathe alien atmospheres, or where humans and aliens can effortlessly make themselves understood in the same language, or even where humans and aliens can reproduce together. Certainly among other science fiction authors in the 1960s there are those who consciously wrote their planets different from Earth – Poul Anderson's *The Man Who Counts* (1958), Hal Clement's Mesklinite trilogy of the 1950s, Larry Niven's Jinx from *The World of Ptavvs* (1966) – but none of these Western writers constructed a world quite so alien as Lem's Solaris. Anderson's, Clement's, and Niven's worlds are all places ultimately understandable to humans, where one must simply learn the rules and differences and then one can get by just fine. Instead, Solaris is unknowable – sure, its poisonous atmosphere can be solved with an environmental suit, but it took solaricists decades of squabbling to conclude it contained intelligent life, much less to communicate with said life. By the end of the novel, humanity is no closer to having solved the mystery of Solaris and its inhabitant. Solaris is one of the least Earth-like worlds in science fiction, and certainly features one of the least human-like aliens. And yet, it is still a mirror, just a self-aware one on Lem's part – a mirror reflecting the hope for a planetary view like Gaia, and the frustration of the sample size problem.

Works such as *Solaris* urge us to view our own planet holistically, as an interconnected system, and to do so with an awareness of our own biases. I have described modern science's current lack of a satisfactory definition for life, which is mirrored in Lem's solaricists taking turns from different disciplinary backgrounds in trying and failing to define how the ocean controls Solaris's orbit, and mirrored again in Lovelock's consideration that rigid disciplinary boundaries hold science back and were the cause of much of the backlash faced by Gaia theory. The planetary view espoused by both *Solaris* and Gaia encourages an interdisciplinary understanding of Earth and all its systems, to include human ones. This vision is being played out in modern exoplanet science, with its frequent study of the Earth as an analogue in preparation for more data on distant exoplanets, and its ongoing awareness of the sample size problem in the search for universal biology. Just as Lem was acutely aware of the perils of anthropomorphism, so too are modern scientists aware of the dangers of an Earth-centric view (as well as their inability to avoid it in some cases). This fundamental understanding that we evolved along with the Earth, that as life of Earth we are part of the Gaia system, is understood implicitly by Lem in his portrayal of human failure to understand another intelligence. While samples of the Solaran ocean wither and die when separated from their whole, humans are more autonomous and can venture out on their own – but life in space, away from the 1-bar of pressure, 1g gravity, and oxygen and nitrogen atmosphere environment we evolved in, wears at us too. *Solaris* is as essential text advocating for interdisciplinarity and self-awareness in the search for life on other worlds.

Works Cited

"ARIEL." *European Space Agency*. https://sci.esa.int/web/ariel. Accessed 23 April 2021.

Baxter, S. "Big Planets: Super-Earths in Science Fiction." *Journal of the British*

Interplanetary Society, vol. 67, 2014, pp. 105-9.

Clarke, Bruce. "The Planetary Imaginary: Gaian Ecologies from *Dune* to *Neuromancer*." *Earth, Life, and System: Evolution and Ecology on a Gaian Planet*, edited by Bruce Clarke, Fordham University Press, 2015, pp. 151-74.

Cortesão, Marta. "What is Life: Various Definitions Toward the Contemporary Astrobiology." *ResearchGate*. 2015. DOI:10.13140/RG.2.1.2618.8002. Accessed 15 April, 2021.

D'Angelo, G., and Bodenheimer, P. "In Situ and Ex Situ Formation Models of Kepler Planets." *The Astrophysical Journal*, vol. 828, 2016, DOI:10.3847/0004-637X/828/1/33.

Federman, Raymond, and Stanisław Lem. "An Interview with Stanisław Lem." *Science Fiction Studies*, vol. 10, no. 1, 1983, pp. 2–14. *JSTOR*, ww.jstor.org/stable/4239523. Accessed 23 April 2021.

Greaves, J.S., Richards, A.M.S., Bains, W. et al. "Phosphine Gas in the Cloud Decks of Venus." *Nature Astronomy*, 2020. https://doi.org/10.1038/s41550-020-1174-4. Accessed 15 April 2021.

Greaves, J.S., Richards, A.M.S., Bains, W. et al. "Re-analysis of Phosphine in Venus' Clouds." *arXiv*, arXiv:2011.08176. Accessed 15 April 2021.

Huang, S. "Life-Supporting Regions in the Vicinity of Binary Systems." *Publications of the Astronomical Society of the Pacific*, vol. 72, no. 425, 1960, pp. 106-14.

Jaime, L.G., Aguilar, L., and Pichardo, B. "Habitable Zones with Stable Orbits for Planets around Binary Systems." *Monthly Notices of the Royal Astronomical Society*, vol. 443, no. 1, 2014, pp. 260–274.

Jemisin, N.K. Hugo Awards, WorldCon 76, 19 August 2018, San Jose. Acceptance Speech.

Le Guin, Ursula K. Introduction. *The Left Hand of Darkness*, 1969. Gollancz, Orion Publishing Group Ltd, 2017, pp. xiii-xvii.

Léger, A., Selsis, F., Sotin, C. et al. "A New Family of Planets? 'Ocean-Planets'." *Icarus*, vol. 169, no. 2, 2004, pp. 499-504.

Lem, Stanisław. *Solaris*, 1961. Translated by Bill Johnston, Pro Auctore Wojciech Zemek, Kindle Edition, 2017.

---. *Summa Technologiae*, 1964. Translated by Joanna Zylinska, University of Minnesota Press, 2013.

Lem, S., Engel, P., and Sigda, J. "An Interview with Stanisław Lem." *The Missouri Review*, vol. 7, no. 2, 1984, pp. 218-37.

Lovelock, J.E. *Gaia: A New Look at Life on Earth*. Oxford University Press, 1979.

---. *The Ages of Gaia: A Biography of our Living Earth*. 2nd ed., Oxford University Press, 2000.

---. *The Vanishing Face of Gaia: A Final Warning*. Penguin, 2009.

Lovelock, J.E., & Giffin, C.E. "Planetary Atmospheres: Compositional and other changes associated with the presence of Life". *Advances in the Astronautical Sciences*, vol. 25, 1969, pp. 179–193.

Margulis, Lynn. *Symbiotic Planet: A New Look at Evolution*. Basic Books, 1998.

NASA Exoplanet Archive. California Institute of Technology, https://exoplanetarchive.ipac.caltech.edu/. Accessed 15 April 2021.

Pak, Chris. *Terraforming: Ecopolitical Transformations and Environmentalism in Science Fiction*. Liverpool University Press, 2016.

Sagan, C. "Life." *Encyclopaedia Britannica*. Encyclopaedia Britannica Incorporated, 1970, pp. 1083-1083A.

Schwieterman, E.W., Kiang, N.Y., Parenteau, M.N. et al. "Exoplanet Biosignatures: A Review of Remotely Detectable Signs of Life." *Astrobiology*, vol. 18, no. 6, 2018, pp. 663-708.

Shapley, H. *Climatic Change: Evidence, Causes, and Effects*. Harvard University Press, 1953.

Snellen, I.A.G., Guzman-Ramirez, L., Hogerheijde, M.R. et al. "Re-analysis of the 267 GHz ALMA Observations of Venus: No Statistically Significant Detection of Phosphine." *Astronomy & Astrophysics*, vol. 644, 2020, L2.

Villanueva, G., Cordiner, M., Irwin, P. et al. "No Phosphine in the Atmosphere of Venus." *arXiv*, arXiv:2010.14305. Accessed 15 April 2021.

"What is an Exoplanet?" *NASA*, https://exoplanets.nasa.gov/what-is-an-exoplanet/in-depth/. Accessed 15 April 2021.

Yaden, D. B., Iwry, J., Slack, K. J. et al. "The Overview Effect: Awe and Self-Transcendent Experience in Space Flight." *Psychology of Consciousness*, vol. 3, no. 1, 2016, pp. 1-11.

Zakariya, N. "Making Knowledge Whole: Genres of Synthesis and Grammars of Ignorance." *Historical Studies in the Natural Sciences*, vol. 42, no. 5, 2012, pp. 432–475. *JSTOR*, www.jstor.org/stable/10.1525/hsns.2012.42.5.432. Accessed 24 Apr. 2021.

Reality as a Fluctuation, Reality as a Singularity: Between Stanisław Lem's Reception of the Universe and *The Investigation*

Filip Świerczyński

The aim of this paper is to consider Stanisław Lem's postulate of stochastic-fluctuating nature of reality with the help of the conceptual apparatus developed by modern physics. The essay is divided into two parts: the first of them is devoted to Lemian reception of the Universe, with particular attention being paid to the statistical impossibilities — *singularities* — which are presented on the basis of the Markov *quasi*-chain, the second turns to the practical use of them by Lem as pretexts-starting points in the framework of plot construction. It also contains an attempt to "examine" the central point of *The Investigation* plot — which itself is a singularity — as rationally as possible, using the tools and concepts of modern science. The paper is intended to answer the question about Lem's view of reality and the Universe, focusing primarily on *The Investigation* (1959), *His Master's Voice* (1968), and *Thus Spoke Lem* (1987/2002) — an extended interview conducted by Stanisław Bereś.

Empiricism in the face of *singularities*. Lemian cosmological receptions

The extremely topical writing of Stanisław Lem (1921–2006) seems to be an amalgam of meta-futurological predictions (Jarzębski 152–153) and diversified, multifaceted probing of the nature of the most complex phenomena — man and the dimensions in which he functions, starting from cultural and technological, through biological and physical, ending with the Universe *in genere*. Lemian quest also includes the power and effectiveness of science and empiricism, although, it should be emphasized, ultimately Lem's thought is far from scientism understood as a belief in the perfection of both of them[1]. Like technology, they *ex natura rei* can gravitate towards it only asymptotically because their creator is equally imperfect, not only morally, but also structurally, human (Bereś and Lem 327–330; Gomułka 51; Lem, *Summa* 297–358; Okołowski 92). It seems that one of the strongest articulations of this statement can be gleaned from *His Master's Voice* (1968):

The process that engendered us — why, pray, must it have been in every respect perfect? Yet neither we nor our philosophers dare consider the idea that the finality and singularity of the existence of our species do not at all imply a perfection under whose aegis the species originated — just as such perfection is not present at the cradle of any individual (Lem, His Master's Voice 15).

According to Hogarth, the protagonist of the novel, humanity is a hunchback who, in ignorance of the fact that it is possible not to be hunchbacked, for thousands of years has sought an indication of a Higher Necessity in his hump, because he will accept any theory but the one that says that his deformity is purely accidental, that no one bestowed it

---

[1]. "One could say that he [Lem — F. Ś.] grew out of scientism as Kant grew out of Hume" (Okołowski 96).

upon him as part of a master plan, that it serves absolutely no purpose, for the thing was determined by the twists and turns of anthropogenesis (Lem, *His Master's Voice* 15).

I do not believe in human perfection (Lem, *His Master's Voice* 133).

The consequence of the limitations of the technological and scientific instrumentation against the immeasurable complexity of the Universe dominated by chance as a "central category," "the feedback factor of any evolutionary process" (Lem, *Filozofia przypadku* 27; cf. Okołowski 292–310), and at the same time the core of the functioning of reality must be the perceptual disfiguration and the cognitive doubt arising from it. Empirically perceived by man reality "becomes a function of chance, purely statistical processes, in which classical causality has ceased to occur" (Drewnowski 437) — Lem's early admiration for Hans Reichenbach, "essentially a secondary philosopher who showed that all knowledge of facts is only probabilistic," noted by Paweł Okołowski, is not surprising then (Okołowski 99; cf. Reichenbach 241). The operation of the machinery of the Universe in the optics available to the human intellect is not ergodic[2] and the curse of dimensionality, "a malediction

---

2. To consider the whole *life* of the Universe within a single aeon — understood in accordance with the definition provided by Penrose ("On the Gravitization of Quantum Mechanics") — as a fully ergodic process would be a kind of *regressus ad infinitum*. Such a process would have to be considered as the web of the Markov chains, which has practically no boundary points and extends to all phenomena occurring in the world. An additional obstacle here is the chaos of deterministic systems, against which even the Laplace's demon remains powerless. On the other hand, Lem, commenting on Douglas Hofstadter's book (*Gödel, Escher, Bach: an Eternal Golden*

that has plagued the scientist from the earliest days" (Bellman 97; cf. Pakes and McGuire), like the sword of Damocles, hangs over it inherently. However, this does not negate the meaningfulness of scientific research — "nothing could be more important than trying to understand where our world is headed" (Lem, *Mój pogląd* 8; cf. Сверчиньски 412). Despite all this, empiricism as a tool is undoubtedly, from the point of view of its power and effectiveness, the closest to perfection:

> *A certain type of culture gave birth to empiricism. [...] We owe her knowledge from various fields — very inspiring and fascinating for me. [...] Empiricism is a kind of powerful launcher into the space of reality. I am deeply convinced that the knowledge it provides is not apparent. [...] If a hypothesis brings instrumental confirmation in the form of material results that can be touched, that can create something, that can heal someone, then there is no more powerful test of its truthfulness. [...] Science has no rivals. [...] Beyond empiricism, I cannot learn anything! Where did humans come from? Where did the Earth and the Sun come from? How does my brain work? What is language? Where am I going as a thinking human being? These are all the questions we discussed in this conversation. Beyond science, there are no answers to them. And if they are, they do not satisfy me.*

Braid, 1979), in an interview with Stanisław Bereś, says: "Its message is very close to me, because it proclaims a cognitive optimistic attitude, that it is not that the whole is irreducible to parts, but actually, if we make a strong effort, we can simplify a lot by reduction. That is pretty comforting" (Bereś and Lem 169).

> *Empiricism is the most modest of all the others. It does not say it knows everything. It admits its mistakes. It emphasizes the extent of its own ignorance. [...] Science does not hide the vastness of its ignorance. [...] I do not see any alternative — I cannot even imagine a culture that would reject empiricism these days. There is no such because it would mean the doom of this culture, throwing it out of the area of the existing world (Bereś and Lem 248–249).*

The more or less apparent norm of the functioning of the Universe is what is the most common and at the same time shows regularity, therefore Lem considers mathematics[3] and physics, and within their framework also statistics, to be the most rooted and embedded in reality sciences (Bereś and Lem 306–350). "A phenomenon is subject to analysis only if the structure of its events, as in this case, conforms to a regular pattern" (Lem, *The Investigation* 119) — states Harvey Sciss, the hero of *The Investigation* (1959), to later add that:

> *So-called common sense relies on programmed nonperception, concealment, or ridicule of everything that doesn't fit into the conventional nineteenth century vision of a world that can be explained down to the last detail. Meanwhile, in actuality you can't*

---

3. Closest to the truth, yet still unreliable: "Genuinely to opt for death, against life, and for mathematics, against the world, is not possible. The only true option is one's own annihilation. Whatever we do, we do in life; and, as experience has demonstrated, neither is mathematics the perfect retreat, because its habitation is language" (Lem, *His Master's Voice* 12).

> *take a step without encountering some phenomenon that you cannot understand and will never understand without the use of statistics (Lem, The Investigation 157).*

"Empirically true" means for Lem "closest to the truth," i.e. "most probable" or "most expected," and the scope of man's research pursuits is "an expanding series whose limit is infinity" (Lem, *His Master's Voice* 29). Phenomena that are virtually unverifiable and have neither rational, statistical, or logical basis nor analogues in the surrounding world — *singularities* — Lem rejects completely or almost completely, assessing their probability as close to zero, as in the case of *quasi*-telepathic interactions (Bereś and Lem 334–336).

There are at least seven postulated or observable, albeit collectively improbable, statistical singularities that science *ipso facto* cannot deny: (1) the initial cosmological singularity or, more generally, the initial moment ($t = 0$), (2) the spontaneous symmetry breaking between matter and antimatter, (3) "biophile" configuration of physical constants established at the very beginning of the hadron epoch (i.e. not later than $t = 10^{-8}$ s) and visible in the present Universe, (4) baryogenesis and primordial nucleosynthesis, (5) accidental density heterogeneities in the initial hydrogen-helium soup evoking the formation of the first molecular clouds, stars, and, consequently, chemical elements having proton number $4 \leq Z$ (including essential nutrients)[4], (6) abiogenesis, and finally (7) the emergence of intelligent life. Together, in a

---

4. Cf. Arnett; Frebel 51–129, 210–240; Hartle 375, 400–401; Heller; Inutstuka et al.; Kartunnen et al. 371–387.

vast simplification, they can be considered on a Markov *quasi*-chain basis — then each singularity 1–7 is understood as a state, i.e. as a universe in which it was realized. The output data, and therefore the probabilities of the individual state transitions, are neither known nor computable. In addition, singularities 6 and 7, due to the absence of traces of extraterrestrial life in any form, can be considered only geo- and anthropocentrically, i.e. from the axiomatically limited perspective of the Earth and man. Consequently, it must be assumed that abiogenesis occurred no earlier than 4.1 billion years ago (the age of oldest rocks found containing biogenic carbon isotopes ^{12}C and ^{13} — Bell et al.; cf. Ohtomo et al.), and the beginnings of intelligent life can be seen no earlier than 3.3 million years ago (the age of the oldest tools found — Harmand et al.).

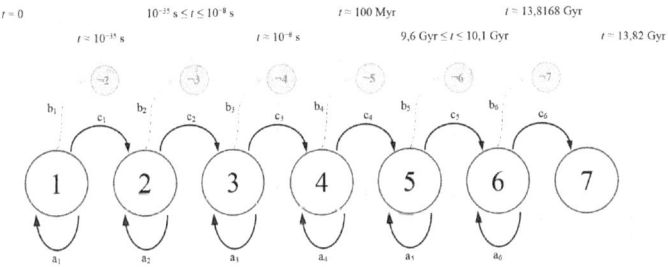

t — the time of the existence of the Universe (from the initial moment to the present)

$a_1, a_2, a_3, a_4, a_5, a_6, a_7$ — the probability of maintaining the *status quo* — no change in state

$b_1, b_2, b_3, b_4, b_5, b_6, b_7$ — the (unknown) probabilities of transitions to all possible (unrealized in the present Universe) states different from 2, 3, 4, 5, 6, 7

$c_1, c_2, c_3, c_4, c_5, c_6, c_7$ — the (unknown) probabilities of transitions to states realized in the present Universe

$1 \to 2 \oplus \neg 2$, $2 \to 3 \oplus \neg 3$, $3 \to 4 \oplus \neg 4$ etc., no pair of states communicate, the states $\neg 2$–$\neg 7$ and 7 are for simplicity absorbing, there are no reflecting boundaries, and in addition, the states 1–6 are temporary (cf. Privault 117–128). To estimate the combined probability of the first two transitions ($1 \to 2 \to 3$), i.e. $c_1 \wedge c_2$ — the probability of an occurring of a universe with as a biophile configuration of physical constants as in the present reality — we can refer to the estimates of Lee Smolin, according to which it is approximately $1:10^{229}$ (Smolin 36–46, 324–326). Even if we assume that the probability of the final formation of celestial bodies and essential nutrients ($3 \to 4 \to 5$, $c_3 \wedge c_4$) for the universe with the current configuration is 1, it is still extremely difficult to estimate the statistical chances of anthropogenesis itself or, more broadly, the emergence of intelligent life and life *in genere* ($5 \to 6 \to 7$, $c_5 \wedge c_6$), although such attempts are being made (Snyder-Beattie et al.; Wilf and Ewens). An apparently helpful tool would seem to be the Drake equation, according to which, depending on the chosen variant (optimistic or pessimistic) and preliminary data, the probability of intelligent life evolution for a single planet or moon in our universe (denoted here as ζ) varies in the following range[5]:

$$\frac{1}{2 \times 10^{18}} \leq \zeta \leq \frac{1}{8 \times 10^{16}}$$

In view of the statistical condition put forward by Adam Frank and Woodruff T. Sullivan (if $\zeta > 1/10^{24}$, then humanity should not consider itself the only technological civilization

---

[5]. Cf. Burchell; Drake and Sobel 55–62; Maccone; Smolyar.

emerged during the existence of the Universe — Frank and Sullivan), *in theoria* fulfilled, we can, taking the optimistic variant, assume that the probability of the emergence of any intelligent life for the universe with the current configuration of physical constants (i.e. transit $5 \to 6 \to 7$, $c_5 \wedge c_6$) is 1. Then, however, the total probability of realization of the last of the links (7) is still close to zero — we still face the initial problem outlined by Smolin, which finds its explanatory reflections both in works based on the theory of the fine-tuned Universe (Waller; Sloan et al.), and in theories of cyclic universes, including Roger Penrose's conformal cyclic cosmology (Penrose, "Before the Big Bang," *Cycles of Time*, "On the Gravitization of Quantum Mechanics"), or the theory of the multiverse (Everett "'Relative State' Formulation," "The Theory of the Universal Wavefunction;" cf. Ben-Dov; Osnaghi et al.). The implication of accepting the first of these theories would have to be the recognition of the postulates of at least a weak variant of the anthropic principle (Barbour 23–25; cf. Heller and Pabjan 195), in turn, the recognition of the second or the third would lead to the conclusion that, statistically, there must have been approximately 10^{229} iterations (consecutive bygone universes) or 10^{229} parallel universes, so that the combination of physical constants has a chance to be regulated as it is now.

Lem rejects both theories associated with cyclic universes:

> *[…] there was a critical moment from which the duration of the Universe could be counted. But there may also be someone who will say that this does not mean that the universe began just then, but that*

something peculiar happened to it. It could have been a part of a more immense whole. It could have just been a metagalactic bladder that suddenly popped up and in which we are in right now. But it may also be that there was something else before, after which there was not even a trace left. Here, however, comes Occam's razor: entities should not be multiplied without necessity. There is no evidence that there was a "something" before, so we assume that there was a "zero" (Bereś and Lem 306–307)[6].

---

6. On the other hand, it is worth remembering that Lem makes it a constitutive component of the plot of *His Master's Voice*: "What begins again to swell spherically and form the expanding Universe is a spreading, globe-shaped neutrino wave, and that wave is at the same time the matrix of creation for all the particles that will occupy the soon-to-be-born Universe; it carries them with it, but only potentially. [...] But when this Universe is in full swing, with its nebulae flung wide, as ours is now, there are still stray echoes in it of the neutrino wave that brought it into being, and this is His Master's Voice! From the gust that forced its way through the 'fissure,' from that neutrino wave arose the atoms, the stars and planets, the nebulae and the metagalaxies. [...] This emission provides a permanent link between the successive worlds, the expiring and the newly created, [...] this neutrino stream is the 'seed' of the next Universe, that this is a kind of metagenesis or alternation of generations, separated by macrocosmic time. [...] Neutrinos are the seeds from disintegration only because, of all the particles, they are the most stable. Their indestructibility guarantees the cyclic return of genesis, its repetitions" (Lem, *His Master's Voice* 181–182). In Lem's thinking and the assumptions of Penrose's conformal cyclic cosmology, one can see excellent similarities — the difference is based on the fact that according to Penrose's theory, it is not neutrinos, but photons, gluons, and postulated gravitons, as massless particles, that can break through the "aeon slit," being the artifacts of the past universe (cf. Penrose, "Before the Big Bang," Cycles of Time, "On the Gravitization of Quantum Mechanics"). About the fact that neutrinos are subject to oscillations, and therefore have mass, Lem naturally could not know (cf. Overbye).

and Hugh Everett's theory of the multiverse:

One tries to save this theory [the Big Bang Theory — F. Ś.] by claiming that as a result of the explosion, not one cosmic bubble was created, but several — ergo, that several universes were created at the same time. [...] This is impossible to verify because you cannot experimentally create the cosmos and check whether this hypothesis is true. From the empirical point of view, this is counter-empirical. [...] From the point of view of empirical orthodoxy, this is already pure metaphysics (Bereś and Lem 308–309).

Instead, Lem turns directly to a more thorough consideration of the anthropic problem:

My honest conviction leads me to say that today there is an increasingly recognizable connection — and it is multidimensional — between the physical properties of the universe and the phenomena of the origin of life. [...] It is not true — as one might think before recognizing these properties of matter — that by something like shuffling cards or throwing dice, i.e. by pure mechanical repetition of random distributions of these improbable combinations of cosmic initial data, abiogenesis could be obtained. That is not the case at all. If at the beginning of cosmogenesis there were even small changes, then abiogenesis would never have occurred. [...] There's a big mystery here. It is no longer possible to agree to the hitherto ontologically neutral, although scientifically correct, model, which proclaims that there is an incredible variety of

> *possible combinations of starting states of cosmos and states of matter. It is not at all the case that if someone plays a cosmic bridge for billions of years, he will eventually get a grand slam in the form of life. For this grand slam to finally come together, after all, certain cards must be given and certain rules of the game must be adopted. It seems that in this game the cards were so handed out, and the conditions when so "thought out" as if it takes into account the possibility of germinating the biogenetic process. I call it a big mystery that I cannot solve. […] Denying personal properties to that which gave birth to the world, I see at the same time a non-randomness and insufficient explanation in the act of postulating here the accidentality of the origin of life, and therefore of man. […] The anthropic factor is not something that an astrophysicist can only tell a child to sleep. There's something to it! […] It is impossible to reduce the origin of life on Earth with man to pure randomness (Bereś and Lem 311–315).*

The birth of a universe with such biophile convergences of physical constants seems to be a central singularity for Lem[7], in the face of which other improbabilities begin to take secondary importance, taking on the semblance of realizable — henceforth, according to this perspective,

---

[7]. "Here, in my ontology and in my thinking, there is a terrible hole. I cannot fill it with anything. Anything! However, this is a dilemma that in ten, fifty, or five hundred years may be apparent. It follows that no man, and therefore I too, can jump out of his skin or out of a historical moment — the horizon of knowledge in which we are trapped is impassable. I am here — I repeat — at the bottom of my ontic thinking" (Bereś and Lem 312).

"everything is possible in this strange world" (Bereś and Lem 282) and physics, colliding with certain phenomena, "announces its collapse because it is not able to predict what is happening" (Bereś and Lem 327), turning into a kind of *post*-empirical metaphysics. Cosmology, *per analogiam*, struggling with statistical distractions, attempts to consider singularities, goes beyond the limits of empiricism, gravitating towards cosmosophy. This is the reason for Lem's reservations about the validity of the theory postulating the primordial spontaneous symmetry breaking:

The fluctuation theory, which assumes that the cosmos arises as a huge violation of nothingness, looks correct and can be reasoned, but there is no chance of its acceptance. There must be some criteria. This conception is improbable elephantiasis of real phenomena, perceived on the smallest scale. […] Everything happens on the border of empiricism if we understand it in the same way as the philosophers of nature did. Logically, then, this theory is correct, but I really do not know by what experience it could be verified (Bereś and Lem 310; cf. Hartle 381; Hartle and Hawking).

Similarly, in *His Master's Voice*, Lem admits in part "some correctness" to reasoning based on considering the world and man as an outcome of stochastic processes:

If we know nothing so well as ourselves, it is surely for this reason: that we constantly renew our demand for nonexistent knowledge, i.e., information as to what created man, while ruling out in advance, without

*realizing it, the possibility of the union of pure
accident with the most profound necessity (Lem, His
Master's Voice 14).*

Ultimately, however, like empiricism, he remains helpless in the face of the central singularity. Nevertheless, he acknowledges that "the utter insignificance and smallness of man *vis-à-vis* the Universe," whose functioning is "a certain play of forces perfectly indifferent to man" (Lem, *His Master's Voice* 11, 25), assuming that trying to solve the initial problem would be tantamount to entering "a labyrinth of possibilities" (Lem, *The Investigation* 130), which is a "fertile ground for ever-proliferating metaphysics" (Lem, *His Master's Voice* 24). It seems that Lem's caution stems from a circumspect awareness — escaping from empiricism we "have to include everything," we intellectually fall into the alogically distorted *circulus vitiosus* and we can believe in everything, and then "the ground opens up beneath our feet, our whole civilization turns into jelly, people can appear and disappear, everything is possible" (Lem, *The Investigation* 139). Crossing the threshold of the "labyrinth of possibilities" is also crossing "the boundary between the definite and the indefinite" where "each of our thoughts seemed about to reveal one of many possible meanings, then vanished, melting away with every desperate effort we made to grasp it fully" — he who pursues understanding will "plunge into a sea of ambiguous details in which he would drown, comprehending nothing even at the end" (Lem, *The Investigation* 50). This is consistent with Lemian axiom that "he who wields the imagination shall perish in the imagination" (Lem, *His Master's Voice* 196). Empiricism reflected in a distorting mirror leads, therefore, ultimately to the attribution of the raison d'être to phantasms. This is the reason why, as Lem writes in *His Master's Voice*, "science, from its very beginning, has been surrounded by a halo of pseudo-science, which rises like steam from various half-educated heads" (Lem, *His Master's Voice* 20). Pareidolia and descrying simulacral convergences in the physical world are within the limits of the *post*-empirical residuum[8] — the scope of its reflections extends from a more or less accurate[9] search for the omnipresent φ, i.e. the golden proportion in nature (cf. Persaud-Sharma and O'Leary), to attempts to fold article physics into pseudosciences such as psionics and orgone theory (Pigliucci and Boudry; cf. Bereś and Lem 268–270).

When we are faced with the question of the central singularity, we are not ultimately faced with a problem, but with a mystery in the sense proposed by Gabriel Marcel. The supreme imperative for us, as for Lem, is the pursuit of truth (Bereś and Lem 247).

A problem is something which I meet, which I find

[8.] It should not be forgotten that some spontaneous illuminations of pure creative thought about seemingly improbable similarities often bear fruit (such as the hypothesis of Hugh Montgomery and Freeman Dyson concerning the relationship between the distances of adjacent zeros of the Riemann zeta function and the eigenvalues of random Hermitian matrices or the coincidences between the distribution of primes and energy levels in the nuclei of heavy elements observed by Dyson — cf. Conrey 348–349; Wolf 198–201).

[9.] The natural structural convergences of some plants developing on the Fibonacci sequence principle has long allowed for generative modeling of nature using, for example, the Lindenmayer system (Prusinkiewicz and Lindenmayer), and in the future, perhaps, they will help to print living plant organisms (cf. Vancauwenberghe et al.).

completely before me, but which I can therefore lay siege to and reduce. But a mystery is something in which I am myself involved, and it can therefore only be thought of as a sphere where the distinction between what is in me and what is before me loses its meaning and initial validity (Marcel 117).

The Investigation: the singularity as a pretext.

Minor singularities are often a pretext to build a plot for Lem and at the same time a starting point for more general reflections on either the issues of culture and technology or the nature of man and the limits of cognition available to him — this applies, *inter alia*, *The Man from Mars* (1946), *Solaris* (1961), *His Master's Voice*, *The Chain of Chance* (1976), and *Fiasco* (1986). Similarly, in the case of *The Investigation*, the core of the plot — the seemingly random and short-lived "revival" of dead bodies — is not a serious prediction or possibility of hypothetical accidents, but rather a direct consequence of *licentia poetica* within the limits of the work, remaining a deliberate amalgam of grotesque, absurd and hyperbole. Like a scholar of Kafka and Nabokov, Lem's scholar must be aware of the writer's game with the reader.

When, in one of the most serious West German SF magazines, two young people tried to write about the *Golem*, it turned out that due to lack of professional preparation, they were unable to draw a line between what should be considered as a hypothesis and what should be considered as an unusual type of fun that Lem invented himself to dazzle his readers (Bereś and Lem 150).

On the other hand, it seems that from the point of view

of the current state of scientific knowledge, the singularity-pretext presented in *The Investigation*, despite a certain distance from the author signaled in later years[10], does not have to be considered as a joke. Its most complete presentation is given presented by the characters themselves:

Some corpses disappeared. How? The evidence suggests they walked away by themselves. [...] They were helped by whatever causes snail shells to be dextrorotatory. But one in every ten million snail shells is sinistrorsal. This is a fact that can be verified statistically. [...] Resurrection? By no means. Don't be ridiculous. The term is used much too loosely. I'm not claiming that the corpses came back to life, with their hearts beating, their brains thinking, the coagulated blood in their veins flowing again. The changes which take place in a dead body are not reversible in that sense. What other sense is there, you ask — the corpses moved around, changed their positions in space. I agree, but the things you're talking about are nothing but facts (Lem, The Investigation 119).

Cancer manifests itself in an organism as chaos; the

---

10. "I am not happy with *The Investigation*, even though it is well written and builds a lot of tension. It is just that the end is to break the genre pattern and climb the high horse, there arose a relativizing philosophy, which shows that it could have been this way or it could have been different. *The Chain of Chance* is better because it is believable. I could believe it myself. Even in terms of naturalism and naive credibility, it has been done better. And my attachment to this idea comes simply from the fact that I have always had a maniacal attitude to what can be done by chance, coincidence, blind luck, or fate" (Bereś and Lem 85).

organism itself, representing order as it is found in the life processes of a living body, is the antithesis of chaos.

> *Under certain conditions, this chaos factor — that is, cancer, or, more accurately, the cancer virus — is mutated, but it remains alive, vegetating in whatever medium is its host. When the victim stops being sick, the virus goes on living in his corpse. Ultimately, it undergoes such a complete transformation that it develops entirely new powers; it changes from a factor that causes chaos to one that tries to create a new kind of order — a kind of posthumous order. In other words, for a specific period of time, it fights against the chaos represented by death and the decomposition of the body that follows death. To do this, the new factor tries to restore the life process in an organism whose body is already dead. When a dead body begins moving around, it's a sign that this process is going on. The moving corpses, in other words, are produced by a weird symbiotic relationship between the living — that is, the mutated virus — and the dead — the corpse itself. […] Sciss mentioned flying saucers, although he tried to be casual about it. He wanted me to know that we may have to look for the answer in outer space. The second variant involves cosmic forces. We're faced with something along the lines of a "first contact" between Earth and a race of people from the stars. It goes this way: there are beings of some kind out there, intelligent but functioning in a manner completely beyond our comprehension. They want to study human beings at*

> *close range, so they send some kind of — information-gathering instruments, let's call them — to Earth, using a method of transportation that we can't understand yet. Maybe the saucers deliver them. The information-collectors are microscopic — invisible for all practical purposes. Once on Earth they ignore living organisms and are directed — programmed would be a better word — only to the dead. Why? [...] How does a mechanic learn about a machine? He starts it up and watches it in operation. The information-collectors do exactly the same thing. They start up some human corpses, getting everything they want to know in the process. If this variant is correct, there are several good reasons why we can't understand the phenomenon. First of all, the information-collector seems to act rationally; therefore, it isn't a device or tool in our sense of the word. It's probably more comparable to a hunting dog: in other words, some kind of trained bacteria (Lem, The Investigation 136–138).*

Partial analogues of the described *factor*, together with the effect it has on the corpse, can be seen both in nature and in the latest achievements of nanotechnology.

Known to modern parasitology, examples of organisms changing the behavior of the host, often in a seemingly arbitrary way, can be enumerated almost indefinitely (cf. Dobson; Moore; Mouritsen and Poulin). The spectrum of possible behavioral modifications extends to making the body of a semi-dead host a kind of a *vehiculum*[11] and

---

11. "'What about the dead animals we found at the scene of the

ultimately leading it to death. The most striking examples include *Paragordius tricuspidatus*, belonging to the phylum *Nematomorpha* and parasitizing, *inter alia*, on crickets, and *Ophiocordyceps unilateralis*, a species of predatory fungus infecting *Camponotus leonardi* ants. The first maximizes the propensity of the host to phototaxis, forcing it to search for a reservoir and most often, indirectly, to drown (Ponton et al.), the second takes control of the muscles of the legs and mandibles of the host, additionally changing its response to pheromones — the fungus, impairing the locomotor system of the ant, forces it to climb a tree, bite hard into a leaf, and then causes its muscles to atrophy, resulting in its death (Andersen et al.; cf. Hughes et al.). Similarly, a wide variety of organisms that modify the host's behavior to increase its susceptibility to predation is known to parasitology, such as *Dicrocoelium dendriticum*, *Euhaplorchis californiensis*, *Toxoplasma gondii*, or *Microphallus piriformes* (Dubey; Lafferty and Morris; McCarthy et al.; Romig et al.).

The very programming of cells or simple living organisms based on DNA or RNA modifications, as well as the construction of fully programmable multicellular biocomputers, has long been part of the scope of nanotechnology (Hopwood). Nowadays, Lemian "trained

---

disappearances?' [...] 'I didn't analyze that particular point mathematically, but the simplest and most fundamental explanation would be to regard the animal as a *vehiculum*, that is to say, as the carrier or medium which conveys the movement factor to the corpse. This factor is specific to a particular biological *agens*; it is similar in nature to whatever causes cancer, and in certain circumstances, we must assume, the *something* that produces cancer is transmuted into our factor; that is, it employs small domestic animals as a means of moving from one place to another. Rats, to cite a well-known example, played the same role in bubonic plague'" (Lem, *The Investigation* 123).

bacteria" are no longer just a hypothetical prediction, but a fact which is confirmed not only by their successfully modified copies (Liu et al.; Shapiro and Gil) or the programming languages intended to train them developed by the company *Asimov*[12] (Trafton) but also by the first primitive computers built of them (Katz; Mogas-Díez et al.; Qiu et al.). An undoubtedly fundamental step for nanotechnology is xenobots — programmable and fully organic nanorobots designed in 2020 by Michael Levin's research team. The construction of Levin's "biological machines" is based on ectoderm and cardiomyocytes formed from stem cells taken from embryos of the frog *Xenopus laevis* in the blastula stage. The cellular architecture of the machines is generated algorithmically *in silico* and the most promising projects are carried out *in vivio* manually using microsurgical instruments. Xenobots also possess autoregenerative abilities. The life of cells in the original version of the experiment was 7–10 days (Kriegsman et al.).

The technical possibilities of the hypothetical realization of the singularity presented in Lem's *The Investigation* seem to be getting closer and closer to being achieved by modern science. In order to explain the *factor* "reviving" dead bodies, it would not be necessary, as it seems, to resort to the explications involving the intervention of extraterrestrial forces — it would be equally possible to assume the action of programmed bacteria or parasites or, on a similar basis, xenobots for one reason or another exploited by a scientist like Wellsian Doctor Moreau (cf. Wells) to move human cadavers. According to this perspective, the

---

12. Link to the project website: https://www.asimov.com/. Accessed 31 May 2021.

singularity presented in *The Investigation* seems to lose the appeal of improbability, and finally — compared to the most absorbing in the world and inherent central singularity — it *omnino* fades. Its realization — as well as the realization of any action — is in a broader perspective a statistically probable stochastic result of the fluctuation-phantom reality, which can be studied successfully only by empiricism — the method that is still the best available, although it is sometimes fallible. The empirical study of reality is, on the one hand, irrevocably entangled with its simplification, on the other hand, it leads to the constant proliferation of unexplored areas, having as the object of analysis a system far from ergodicity. Thus, according to Lem, scientific truths, patched up by statistics, can be read as approximations of real and human-independent truths. The fullest expression of the ontological uncertainty, the metaphorically articulated summary of Lem's thoughts, which is at the same time an accurate summary of the concepts that we have tried to present here, is finally found in one of the closing paragraphs of *The Investigation*, which we quote below, leaving the final word to the author himself.

> *What if the world isn't scattered around us like a jigsaw puzzle — what if it's like a soup with all kinds of things floating around in it, and from time to time some of them get stuck together by chance to make some kind of whole? What if everything that exists is fragmentary, incomplete, aborted, events with ends but no beginnings, events that only have middles, things that have fronts or rears but not both, with us constantly making categories, seeking out, and*

reconstructing, until we think we can see total love, total betrayal and defeat, although in reality we are all no more than haphazard fractions. Our faces and our fates are shaped by statistics — we human beings are the resultant of Brownian motion — incomplete sketches, randomly outlined projections. Perfection, fullness, excellence are all rare exceptions — they occur only because there is such an excess, so unimaginably much of everything! The daily commonplace is automatically regulated by the world's vastness, its infinite variety; because of it, what we see as gaps and breaches complement each other; the mind, for its own self-preservation, finds and integrates scattered fragments. Using religion and philosophy as the cement, we perpetually collect and assemble all the garbage comprised by statistics in order to make sense out of things, to make everything respond in one unified voice like a bell chiming to our glory. But it's only soup…The mathematical order of the universe is our answer to the pyramids of chaos. On every side of us we see bits of life that are completely beyond our understanding — we label them unusual, but we really don't want to acknowledge them. The only thing that really exists is statistics. The intelligent person is the statistical person. Will a child be beautiful or ugly? Will he enjoy music? Will he get cancer? It's all decided by a throw of the dice. At the very moment of our conception — statistics! Statistics determine which clusters of genes our bodies will be created from, statistics determine when we're going to die. A normal

> *statistical distribution decides everything: whether I'm going to meet a woman and fall in love, how long I'm going to live, maybe even whether I'm going to be immortal. From time to time, it may be, statistics participate in some things blindly, by accident — beauty and lameness, for example. But explicit processes will cease to exist before long: soon even despair, beauty, happiness, and ugliness will result from statistics. Our knowledge is underlined by statistics — nothing exists except blind chance, the eternal arrangement of fortuitous patterns. An infinite number of Things taunt our fondness for Order. Seek, and ye shall find; in the end ye shall always find, if you only look with enough fervor; statistics doesn't exclude anything, and therefore it renders everything possible, or more or less probable. History, on the other hand, comes true by Brownian motion, a statistical dance of particles that never stop dreaming about another temporal world...(Lem, The Investigation 204–205).*

Works Cited

Andersen, Sandra B., Gerritsma, Sylvia, Yusah, Kalsum M., Mayntz, David, Hywel-Jones, Nigel L., Billen, John, Boomsma, Jacobus J., Hughes, David P. "The Life of a Dead Ant: The Expression of an Adaptive Extended Phenotype." *American Naturalist*, vol. 174, no. 3, 2009, pp. 424–433.

Arnett, W. David. *Supernovae and Nucleosynthesis: An Investigation of the History of Matter, from the Big Bang to the Present*. Princeton UP, 1996.

Barbour, Julian B. *The End of Time: The Next Revolution in Our Understanding of the Universe*. Oxford UP, 1999.

Bell, Elizabeth A., Boehnke, Patrick, Harrison, T. Mark, Mao,

Wendy L. "Potentially Biogenic Carbon Preserved in a 4.1 Billion-Year-Old Zircon." *Proceedings of the National Academy of Sciences*, vol. 112, no. 47, 2015, pp. 14518–14521.

Bellman, Richard E. *Adaptive Control Process: A Guided Tour*. Princeton UP, 1961.

Ben-Dov, Yoav. "Everett's Theory and the 'Many-Worlds' Interpretation." *American Journal of Physics*, vol. 58, no. 9, 1990, pp. 829–832.

Bereś, Stanisław, Lem, Stanisław. *Tako rzecze Lem. Ze Stanisławem Lemem rozmawia Stanisław Bereś*. Wydawnictwo Literackie, 2018.

Burchell, Mark J. "W(h)ither the Drake Equation?" *International Journal of Astrobiology*, vol. 5, no. 3, 2006, pp. 243–250.

Conrey, J. Brian. "The Riemann Hypothesis," *Notices of the AMS*, vol. 50, no. 3, 2003, pp. 341–353.

Dobson, Andrew P. "The Population Biology of Parasite-Induced Changes in Host Behavior." *The Quarterly Review of Biology*, vol. 63, 1988, pp. 139–165.

Drake, Frank, Sobel, Dava. *Is Anyone Out There? The Scientific Search for Extraterrestrial Intelligence*. Delacorte Press, 1992.

Drewnowski, Tadeusz. *Próba scalenia. Obiegi – wzorce – style. Literatura polska 1944–1989*. Polskie Wydawnictwo Naukowe, 1997.

Dubey, Jitender P. "Infectivity and Pathogenicity of Toxoplasma Gondii Oocysts for Cats." *The Journal of Parasitology*, vol. 82, no. 6, 1996, pp. 957–961.

Everett, Hugh. "'Relative State' Formulation of Quantum Mechanics." *Reviews of Modern Physics*, vol. 29, no. 3, 1957, pp. 454–462.

Everett, Hugh. "The Theory of the Universal Wavefunction." *The Many-Worlds Interpretation of Quantum Mechanics*, edited by Bryce DeWitt, Neill Graham, Princeton UP, 1973, pp. 3–140.

Frank, Adam, Sullivan, Woodruff T. "A New Empirical Constraint on the Prevalence of Technological Species in the Universe." *Astrobiology*, vol. 16, no. 5, 2016, pp. 369–362.

Frebel, Anna. *Searching for the Oldest Stars: Ancient Relics from the Early Universe*. Translated by Ann Hentschel, Princeton UP, 2015.

Gomułka, Łukasz. "O krytyce kultury wg Stanisława Lema." *Humanum. Międzynarodowe studia społeczno-humanistyczne*, no. 24, 2017, pp. 45–54.

Harmand, Sonia, Lewis, Jason E., Feibel, Craig S., Lepre,

Christopher J., Prat, Sandrine, Lenoble, Arnaud, Boës, Xavier, Quinn, Rhonda L., Brenet, Michel, Arroyo, Adrian, Taylor, Nicholas, Clément, Sophie, Daver, Guillaume, Brugal, Jean-Philip, Leakey, Louise, Mortlock, Richard A., Wright, James D., Lokorodi, Sammy, Kirwa, Christopher, Kent, Dennis V., Roche, Hélène. "3.3-Million-Year-Old Stone Tools From Lomekwi 3, West Turkana, Kenya." *Nature*, vol. 521, 2015, pp. 310–315.

Hartle, Jim B. *Gravity: An Introduction to Einstein's General Relativity*. Addison-Wesley, 2003.

Hartle, Jim B., Hawking, Stephen W. "Wave Function of the Universe." *Physical Review D*, vol. 29, no. 12, 1983, pp. 2960–2975.

Heller, Michał, Pabjan, Tadeusz. *Elementy filozofii przyrody*. Copernicus Center Press, 2014.

Heller, Michał. "Cosmological Singularity and the Creation of the Universe." *Zygon: Journal of Religion and Science*, vol. 35, no. 3, 2000, pp. 665–685.

Hopwood, David A. "The Genetic Programming of Industrial Microorganisms." *Scientific American*, vol. 245, no. 3, 1981, pp. 90–105.

Hughes, David P., Andersen, Sandra B., Hywel-Jones, Nigel L., Himaman, Winanda, Billen, Johan, Boomsma, Jacobus J. "Behavioral Mechanisms and Morphological Symptoms of Zombie Ants Dying from Fungal Infection." *BMC Ecology*, vol. 11, 2011, ID 13.

Inutstuka, Shu-ichiro, Inoue, Tsuyoshi, Iwasaki, Kazunari, Hosokawa, Takashi. "The Formation and Destruction of Molecular Clouds and Galactic Star Formation. An Origin for the Cloud Mass Function and Star Formation Efficiency." *Astronomy & Astrophysics*, vol. 580, 2015, A49.

Jarzębski, Jerzy. *W Polsce czyli wszędzie: szkice o polskiej prozie współczesnej*. PEN, 1992.

Kartunnen, Hannu, Kröger, Pekka, Oja, Heikki, Poutanen, Markku, Donner, Karl J. *Fundamental Astronomy*. Springer, 2003.

Katz, Evgeny, editor. *DNA- and RNA-Based Computing Systems*. Wiley-VCH, 2021.

Kriegman, Sam, Blackiston, Douglas, Levin, Michael, Bongard, Josh. "A Scalable Pipeline for Designing Reconfigurable Organisms." *Proceedings of the National Academy of Sciences of the United States of America*, vol. 117, no. 4, 2020, pp. 1853–1859.

Lafferty, Kevin D., Morris, A. Kimo. "Altered Behavior of Parasitized Killifish Increases Susceptibility to Predation by Bird Final Hosts." *Ecology*, vol. 77, no. 5, 1996, pp. 1390–1397.

Lem, Stanisław. *Filozofia przypadku. Literatura w świecie empirii*, Agora, 2010.

Lem, Stanisław. *His Master's Voice*. Translated by Michael Kandel, Harcourt Brace Jovanovich, 1983.

Lem, Stanisław. *Mój pogląd na literaturę. Rozprawy i szkice*. Wydawnictwo Literackie, 2003.

Lem, Stanisław. *Summa Technologiae*. Translated by Joanna Żylińska, University of Minnesota Press, 2013.

Lem, Stanisław. *The Investigation*. Translated by Adele Milch, The Seabury Press, 1974.

Liu, Zdeao, Zhang, Jizhong, Jin, Jiao, Geng, Zilong, Qi, Qingsheng, Liang, Quanfeng. "Programming Bacteria With Light — Sensors and Applications in Synthetic Biology." *Frontiers in Microbiology*, vol. 9, 2018, ID 2692.

Maccone, Claudio. "The Statistical Drake Equation." *Acta Astronautica*, vol. 67, 2010, pp. 1366–1383.

Marcel, Gabriel. *Being and Having*. Translated by Katharine Farrer, Dacre Press, 1949.

McCarthy, Helen O., Fitzpatrick, Susan, Irwin, Sam W. B. "Life History and Life Cycles: Production and Behavior of Trematode Cercariae in Relation to Host Exploitation and Next-Host Characteristics." *The Journal of Parasitology*, vol. 88, no. 5, 2002, pp. 910–918.

Mogas-Díez, Sira, Gonzalez-Flo, Eva, Macía, Javier. "2D Printed Multicellular Devices Performing Digital and Analogue Computation." *Nature Communications*, vol. 12, 2021, ID 1679.

Moore, Janice. *Parasites and the Behavior of Animals*. Oxford UP, 2002.

Mouritsen, Kim N., Poulin, Robert. "Parasite-Induced Trophic Facilitation Exploited by a Non-Host Predator: a Manipulator's Nightmare." *International Journal for Parasitology*, vol. 33, 2003, pp. 1043–1050.

Ohtomo, Yoko, Kakegawa, Takeshi, Ishida, Akizumi, Nagase, Toshiro, Rosing, Minik T. "Evidence for Biogenic Graphite in Early Archaean Isua Metasedimentary Rocks." *Nature Geoscience*, vol. 7, no. 1, 2014, pp. 25–28.

Okołowski, Paweł. *Materia i wartości. Neolukrecjanizm Stanisława Lema*. Wydawnictwo Uniwersytetu Warszawskiego, 2010.

Osnaghi, Stefano, Freitas, Fábio, Freire, Olival. "The Origin of the

Everettian Heresy." *Studies in History and Philosophy of Science Part B: Studies in History and Philosophy of Modern Physics*, vol. 40, no. 2, 2009, pp. 97–123.

Overbye, Dennis. "Physics Nobel Is Awarded for Work on Neutrinos." *The New York Times*, 7 Oct. 2015, p. 3.

Pakes, Ariel, McGuire, Paul. "Stochastic Algorithms, Symmetric Markov Perfect Equilibrium, and the 'Curse' of Dimensionality." *Econometrica*, vol. 69, no. 5, 2001, pp. 1261–1281.

Penrose, Roger. "Before the Big Bang: An Outrageous New Perspective and its Implications for Particle Physics." *Proceedings of the 10th European Particle Accelerator Conference, Edinburgh, Scotland, 2006*, edited by Caterina Biscari, Hywel Owen, Christine Petit-Jean-Genaz, John Poole, John Thomason, EPS-AG, 2006, pp. 2759–2762.

Penrose, Roger. "On the Gravitization of Quantum Mechanics 2: Conformal Cyclic Cosmology." *Foundations of Physics*, vol. 44, 2014, pp. 873–890.

Penrose, Roger. *Cycles of Time: An Extraordinary New View of the Universe*. The Bodley Head, 2010.

Persaud-Sharma, Dharam, O'Leary, James P. "Fibonacci Series, Golden Proportions, and the Human Biology." *Austin Journal of Surgery*, vol. 2, no. 5, 2015, p. 1066.

Pigliucci, Massimo, Boudry, Maarten, editors. *Philosophy of Pseudoscience: Reconsidering the Demarcation Problem*. The University of Chicago Press, 2013.

Ponton, Fleur, Otálora-Luna, Fernando, Lefèvre, Thierry, Guerin, Patrick M., Lebarbenchon, Camille, Duneau, David, Biron, David G., Thomasa, Frédéric. "Water-Seeking Behavior in Worm-Infected Crickets and Reversibility of Parasitic Manipulation." *Behavioral Ecology*, vol. 22, no. 2, 2011, pp. 392–400.

Privault, Nicolas. *Understanding Markov Chains*. Springer, 2013.

Prusinkiewicz, Przemysław, Lindenmayer, Aristid. *The Algorithmic Beauty of Plants*. Springer, 2012.

Qiu, Meikang, Khisamutdinov, Emil, Zhao, Zhengyi, Pan, Cheryl, Choi, Jeong-Woo, Leontis, Neocles B., Guo, Peixuan. "RNA Nanotechnology for Computer Design and in Vivo Computation." *Philosophical Transactions of the Royal Society A: Mathematical, Physical and Engineering Sciences*, vol. 37, no. 2000, 2013, ID 20120310.

Reichenbach, Hans. *The Rise of Scientific Philosophy*. University of

California Press, 1951.

Romig, Thomas, Lucius, Richard, Werner, Frank. "Cerebral Larvae in the Second Intermediate Host of *Dicrocoelium Dendriticum* (Rudolphi, 1819) and *Dicrocoelium Hospes* Looss, 1907 (Trematodes, Dicrocoeliidae)." *Zeitschrift Für Parasitenkunde*, vol. 63, 1980, pp. 277–286.

Shapiro, Ehud, Gil, Binyamin. "RNA Computing in a Living Cell." *Science*, vol. 322, no. 5900, 2008, pp. 387–388.

Sloan, David, Batista, Rafael A., Hicks, Michael T., Davies, Roger, editors. *Fine-Tuning in the Physical*. Cambridge UP, 2020.

Smolin, Lee. *The Life of Cosmos*. Oxford UP, 1997.

Smolyar, Daniel. "Communicating with Extraterrestials." *Journal of the Washington Academy of Sciences*, vol. 85, no. 2, 1998, pp. 212–215.

Snyder-Beattie, Andrew E., Sandberg, Anders, Drexler, K. Eric, Bonsall, Michael B. "The Timing of Evolutionary Transitions Suggests Intelligent Life is Rare." *Astrobiology*, vol. 21, no. 3, 2021, pp. 265–278.

Trafton, Anne. "A Programming Language for Living Cells. New Language Lets Researchers Design Novel Biological Circuits." *Massachusetts Institute of Technology News Office*, 31 Mar. 2016, https://news.mit.edu/2016/programming-language-living-cells-bacteria-0331. Accessed 31 May 2021.

Vancauwenberghe, Valérie, Mbong, Victor B. M., Vanstreels, Els, Verboven, Pieter, Lammertyn, Jeroen, Nicolai, Bart. "3D Printing of Plant Tissue for Innovative Food Manufacturing: Encapsulation of Alive Plant Cells Into Pectin Based Bio-Ink." *Journal of Food Engineering*, vol. 263, 2019, pp. 454–464.

Waller, Jason. *Cosmological Fine-Tuning Arguments. What (if Anything) Should We Infer from the Fine-Tuning of Our Universe for Life?* Routledge, 2019.

Wells, Herbert G. *The Island of Doctor Moreau*. CreateSpace, 2014.

Wilf, Herbert S., Ewens, Warren J. "There's Plenty of Time for Evolution." *Proceedings of the National Academy of Sciences of the United States of America*, vol. 107, no. 52, 2010, pp. 22454–22456.

Wolf, Marek. "Spojrzenie fizyka na hipotezę Riemanna." *Wiadomości Matematyczne*, no. 51 (2), 2015, pp. 189–217.

Сверчиньски, Филип. "Между катастрофизмом и пацифизмом: идейные пути Олдоса Хаксли и Станислава Лема." *Пятые Лемовские чтения. Сборник материалов Международной научной конференции памяти Станислава Лема, 5–7 ноября 2020 г.*, отв. ред. Александр Ю. Нестеров, Самарская гуманитарная академия, 2020, pp. 406–418. // Sverchin'ski, Filip. "Mezhdu katastrofizmom i patsifizmom: ideynyye puti Oldosa Khaksli i Stanislava Lema." *Pyatyye Lemovskiye chteniya. Sbornik materialov Mezhdunarodnoy nauchnoy konferentsii pamyati Stanislava Lema, 5–7 noyabrya 2020 g.*, otv. red. Aleksandr Yu. Nesterov, Samarskaya gumanitarnaya akademiya, 2020, pp. 406–418.

Literary Expressions of Nonexistence in Stanislaw Lem and in Italo Calvino: "The Third Sally, or the Dragons of Probability" and The Nonexistent Knight

Pablo Contursi
(Translated by Romina Propato)

Introduction

Let us think of the following question to be our starting point for this work: Which is the relationship, if any, between the short story "The Third Sally, or the Dragons of Probability" (Wyprawa trzecia, czyli smoki prawdopodobieństwa, 1965)[1] by Stanislaw Lem and the short novel *The Nonexistent Knight* (*Il cavaliere inesistente*, 1959) by Italo Calvino?

A quick answer could be that there is actually a quite clear connection between Lem's and Calvino's texts. To begin with, in the versions that we have analyzed (translations by Archibald Colquhoun and Michael Kandel, respectively) this connection is shown through some language components that both texts have in common, such as the noun "nonexistence" and the verb "(to) not exist".

---

[1]. The short story "The Third Sally" was published in Polish in the book *Cyberiada* (Wydawnictwo Literackie, 1965). Another collection of robot stories is *Fables for Robots* (*Bajki Robotów*, Wydawnictwo Literackie, 1964). The later editions of these books, in English (and also in Spanish), changed their content and titles, some texts were added, some were removed. For further information about this, check Keller (25).

These terms share lexical components and are preceded by negative particles or prefixes that reverse their meaning. In both texts, the so-called "nonexistence" plays a key role in the narrative development.

Let us now dig a little bit deeper into this. Trurl and Klapaucius (the two robot protagonists of Lem's *The Cyberia*,) are fighting against dragons which do not exist, but these dragons anyway manage to attack rural areas, howling and throwing fire up in the air –the usual for this legendary and mischievous sort of varmint. And Agilulf, the main character in Calvino's novel, is a knight who, despite having some special virtues (or perhaps, due to the superhuman condition of those virtues) does not exist either –a fact stated by himself in the first pages of the narration. Just like the dragons in "The Third Sally", he appears challenge us with a set of elusive ideas.

The "nonexistent object" (Reicher) and the denotation of an empty set (Lyons 231) are concepts that involve (both in philosophy and linguistics) some old human concerns – much older than the publishing date of "The Third Sally" and *The Nonexistent Knight*. Not only do these ideas, as well as other concepts and terms used in order to think about the partial or total absence or lack of something (such as nothingness, non-being and others) contribute to keeping those dedicated to philosophy, linguistics and cosmology (and religion too) awake at night – but they might also lead us, as readers of literature, to experience a particular esthetic reaction of astonishment. Said astonishment arises from the fact that, no matter how much thought we devote to nothingness, it is not easy to grasp (Barrow xiii, 1).

If we continue checking the correlation between "The

Third Sally" and *The Nonexistent Knight*, we will also find significant contrasts. Thus, the differences related to the way in which nonexistence is depicted in these two fictional worlds are going to highlight some aspects to be considered in order to analyze how Lem and Calvino, each in their own, unique way, imagine stories where that concept (the nonexistence) appears in fiction to illuminate the current situation of humanity on the planet Earth. If, as Elana Gomel states concerning posthumanism, "(t)raditional definitions of humanity are being undermined by advances in science and technology, social and political upheavals, and ideological shifts" (4), the nonexistence of Agilulf and the dragons of probability might be a hint of a crisis in the human conception of their own identity as a species.

The creatures, objects and setting in these stories, as well as in any other narrative fiction, are disclosed to us, readers, through language. That is why outlining a brief theoretical framework on semiology, linguistics and philosophy will provide some overall guidelines to help us track where these fictional productions are located –at the crossroads between language and reality, at the intriguing interspaces between the sign and the actual thing.

Moreover, the truth is that, if we consider the filiation of these two narrative texts with the tradition of the *contes philosophiques* by Swift and Voltaire (Suvin "To Remember Stanislaw Lem" 34; Cavallaro 18-19), it won't appear fully absurd to feel that, as we read them, we are being invited to look at the world with a critical eye. Carl Freedman states that Lem's philosophical satire, under which *The Cyberiad* is classified, in his opinion, "attempts to problematize the epistemological assumptions of unreflective, precritical common sense" (96). In this sense, *The Nonexistent Knight* questions, according to Dani Cavallaro, "the ambitions of rationalist philosophy and historiography alike (…) through the juxtaposition of hyperrational attitudes and utterly illogical situations". (22).

Regarding Lem's works, it has been said that they "explore the ramifications of encounter with the totally Other" (Gomel 187-8). We claim that these narrative texts by Lem and Calvino do the same thing, but with a few evocative particularities. The "nonexistence" may constitute the strangest element in literature –an Absolute Other who, embodied in nonexistent characters, objects, places or times, can break with the literary convention which should be (following proper reasoning) complied with by all genres: in a fiction world, nonexistent creatures and objects should not interact with existing creatures or objects within the same fiction. We state, then, that the defining feature of these literary works is their display of an embodiment where nonexistence and otherness are connected to express the dimension of astonishment –how the *Homo sapiens* feels at looking at their reflection in the twentieth century mirror. Developing some formulations around these topics is going to be the main goal of this writing.

Below, a succinct introduction to Lem and Calvino.

Lem and Calvino
One era, two writers and their diverse and distinct creations

Not only for their incredibly imaginative literary works, but also for the quality of their discerning essay-like contributions (Suvin, "Lem" 712; Cavallaro 3), Stanislaw Lem (1921-2006) and Italo Calvino (1923-1985) are two very distinct writers, while, at the same time, they can be compared with each other. Let me explain: their creations stand out for what we might call an "unmistakable diversity" –their writings are lavish with approaches, speech genres, styles and topics (Swirski, "The Man Behind the Giant" 4; Cavallaro 3). This is a feature that links them both, as it also differentiates them from many other authors. However, their books have followed different directions as regards the interest they aroused among the audience and within different intellectual communities and critics in major countries. In 1985, when he passed away, Calvino was already greatly renowned in the English-speaking world: he was "the best-known and most-translated Italian contemporary author" (McLaughlin xii). The "occidental" popularity of Lem, instead, was cemented a bit later, and if Peter Swirski in 2006 (the year of Lem's death) said that by those days Lem was no longer the "obscure East European writer" (Swirski "The Man Behind the Giant" 3) it was not because he was unknown beyond the Iron Curtain. Quite on the contrary, Lem was well reputed there (in West Germany likewise); his books had been translated and sold out (even in English). Yet, the fact that he was exclusively linked to one genre resulted in, as it usually happens, being identified as a SF reference example (as this is the genre we have been talking about) — rather unreasonably, to our judgment. Curiously enough, nobody would think of classifying Calvino as a SF writer, even though he is the author of books such as *Cosmicomics* and *T Zero*[2]... Be that as it may, despite admitting that Lem has more chances to be considered a

---

2. About this, and about how a "canonical" reading of Calvino's work (far from any link to science fiction) was sponsored by himself and by Eugenio Montale, see Baldi.

generic SF writer than Calvino, it does not mean that there is still a necessary verification missing: we are talking about the appreciation of Stanislaw Lem as one of the major writers of the twentieth century.[3]

In the next section, we will place "The Third Sally" and *The Nonexistent Knight* within the body of works written by each author.

"The Third Sally" and *The Nonexistent Knight*
A short-story, a novel, two literary cycles

"The Third Sally, or the Dragons of Probability", by Stanislaw Lem, is one of the stories of the set "The Seven Sallies of Trurl and Klapaucius", included in the book *The Cyberiad* (*Cyberiada*, 1965). In the short story, some nonexistent dragons start causing problems on several planets of the Galaxy, and the robots Trurl and Klapaucius (the constructors) are required to solve them. As it happens with most fictions by Lem ("An Interview with Stanislaw Lem"), here the well-intentioned actions of the characters result in a big mess that they try to solve later on. The problems (that is to say, the dragons) emerge from scientific experimentation and the pursuit of knowledge; this topic, as we know, is considered one of the typical features of modern science fiction literature (remember Mary Shelley's *Frankenstein*). What makes *The Cyberiad* stand out from the Lemian works is the concurrence of elements that appear scattered in some other books of his. It is humor (distinctive

---

[3]. There are a few exceptions. In 2006 Darko Suvin would refer to him as "a distinctive and major voice in world literature" ("To Remember Stanislaw Lem" 34) and Peter Swirski as "one of the greatest writers and thinkers of the twentieth century and beyond" (*Philosopher of the Future* 3). One year earlier, Fredric Jameson regarded Lem as a "great Polish novelist" (Jameson 107).

in *The Star Diaries* and in *Fables for Robots*), satire (present in the latter and in *A Perfect Vacuum*) and the grotesque (decisive in "Do You Exist, Mr. Jones?") which adds to one of the key literary trends in Lem: the one which works "to estrange many of the most taken-for-granted assumptions that govern everyday life" (Freedman 96). However, it would be inappropriate to label these stories as "SF"; as this author mentions, it might be smarter to think that they deal with "themes familiar to science fiction" instead of being made up of examples of this genre strictly speaking (98). In any case, Trurl and Klapaucius are "inhuman" characters who satirize — just as Agilulf does — some human (too human) vanities (Barnouw 156-7).

On the other hand, Italo Calvino has written a set of novels which, by the general name of *Our Ancestors*, is formed by three texts: *The Cloven Viscount* (*Il visconte dimezzato*, 1952), *The Baron in the Trees* (*Il barone rampante*, 1957) and *The Nonexistent Knight* (*Il cavaliere inesistente*, 1959). The latter narrates the adventures of Agilulf, a nonexistent knight who is, however, able to carry out great feats that turn him into an ephemeral hero in the Army of Charlemagne. According to Calvino's own words in his prologue to the Italian edition of the trilogy, the contemporary man "is divided, mutilated, incomplete, enemy to himself" (Hume 50), a description which, of course, fits perfectly the protagonist of *The Cloven Viscount*, but also th the characters after which the other two novels are named. Both the "repression" diagnosed by Freud in the modern subject and the "alienation" claimed by Marx in his materialist analysis of society are embodied in that nonexistent knight and in that Baron who decides to isolate himself from his peers and live up in the trees (if we are not misled by Calvino's words). Agilulf is an anachronic representative of these psychological and socioeconomic conflicts, which actually do not belong in the Middle Age but in the twentieth and twenty-first centuries. A state of continuing conflict with himself and with the others (his unhealthy impenetrability, his perfectionism, his inability to love) prevents him from balancing his overwhelming willingness to fight for a noble cause with the "inner emptiness" that literally inhabits him (Weiss 39). His wishes and urges, obsessive and drawing near arrogance, keep him active until the narration finally does away with him.

Next, we're going to review some theoretical concepts about signs and knowledge. The idea is to have a quick look at the limits between language and comprehension.

Facing the limits: signs and knowledge
The enigmatic nonexistence

What are we talking about when we mention nonexistent creatures or objects?

The topic of nonexistence can be framed within a wide tradition of the occidental culture (as well as the oriental culture)[4]. Just think that nonexistence, along with some other terms or concepts with related semantic content (nothingness, non-being, nihilism, negation, negativity, emptiness, void,

---

4. It is not even possible to try to deal with this topic here, not even superficially. Suffice it to say that in Occident the systematic reflection about these "negative" concepts start with the old Greek philosophers (Bakaoukas), but there were others in Mathematics (since the invention of zero, for example). In the Oriental world there is an important tradition of reflections and beliefs about similar matters: Buddhist philosopher Nagarjuna (to mention just one) dedicated to dig into the notion of "voidness"; for more information about him, see Fatone and Dragonetti and Tola.

vacuum), has been accompanying humans for centuries (Bakaoukas, Déprez and Espinal). In some cases, the elements of this "negative conceptual body" work as the components of a communication system of daily use (negation in natural language, Horn xiii). In other cases, they work as abstract objects of the philosophical reflection or as religious beliefs; and yet in other cases, as scientific notions that attempt to explain the physical reality[5]. Within philosophy, the area of the "nonexistent objects" has gained renewed importance quite recently, as well as the studies about fiction and fictional entities (Everett 1).

The total nothingness and nonexistence are beyond the human experience. At least, we cannot experience them fully or truly while we are alive. What we can do is feel an indirect or partial impact: the death of other beings, their absence, their disappearance –and the degradation of material and living things, which feels rather like a reflection or a shadow or the echo of that which exists within us only in the form of thoughts (maybe that which *more than anything else* exists in our minds only in the form of thoughts).

As mentioned earlier, another concern we'd like to tackle is the link between world and language. For semiology and semantics, one of the key problems of the referential function (or "denotation") is naming the objects with which language communication refers to objects from the extra-

---

5. We're not stating that there is an identity or equivalent concept between these disciplines. For more about nihilism, see Crosby. For more about the zero as a human invention and object of Mathematics, and about the void or vacuum as object of physical sciences, see Barrow. For more about nonexistence and philosophical approaches from fiction and related concepts, see Everett. The above-mentioned Horn studies negation from language philosophy and logic; and Déprez and Espinal do so from several areas of Linguistics.

linguistic reality (Ducrot and Todorov 247). This means focusing on the "referent", one of the three elements of the classic triangle of meaning –also formed by "symbol" and "thought" (Ogden and Richards 11). ("Signifier" and "signified" are the terms coined by Saussure matching these notions). Although it is a useful and informative outline, this triangle is not valid for all cases: language is far more complex than that.

For instance, even when denotation may help us recall objects of the world (or more specifically, some kinds of objects) (Lyons 78), it won't be always something specific, made of material stuff. Denotation does not necessarily declare the existence of what is denoted; a clear example of this is the fact that we can talk about "fairies" or write about "goblins" and that won't bring those entities into existence. In semantics, the section of linguistics that studies the meaning of words, some experts make a distinction between denotation and reference. In John Lyons' own words (299):

Reference is intrinsically connected with existence; one cannot successfully refer to something that does not exist. One can, of course, successfully refer to imaginary, fictional and hypothetical entities; but in so doing, one presupposes that they exist in an imaginary, fictional or hypothetical world.

This author says that, with the help of the set theory it is possible to denote an empty set, containing, for example, the entities "unicorn" and "centaur" (Lyons 231).

And this leads us to the philosophical problem of the "nonexistent objects". According to what we've been arguing, the connection between words and reality, even when it feels transparent, agile and coherent, is actually far from that. Some issues get magnified in such a paradoxical way if we leave the study of signs behind and think of other more world-oriented disciplines (and less oriented to the codes that we use to talk about the world). In the case of "nonexistence", we might unravel the mystery as to whether a sign, as such, does count or does not count on a referent. From a human viewpoint, the ideas of nonexistence, nothingness, non-being, etc. are not easy to grasp; it seems that the world does not provide particularly clear examples of inexistent objects. According to a first approach, if they are inexistent, then they would not be objects.

Then, let us think of the following question: what about nonexistent objects? Do they have a referent or not? The point is that both an affirmative and a negative answer would bring about some problems. What object to be described under the name of "nonexistent object" shall we find in the world? We won't find unicorns, even if we try hard. But on the other hand, wouldn't just anything or any being that does not exist in this world (a unicorn, for instance) be a "nonexistent object"?

In philosophy, affirmative or negative answers to these questions have led to subsequent problems which are hard to deal with due to their rather evasive resolve. It may seem obvious to state that "there are some nonexistent things" is not just sensible but true. However, the doubts aroused by this topic will not fade out so easily. To this regard, Maria Reicher says in the introduction to "Nonexistent Objects" of the *Stanford Encyclopedia of Philosophy*:

One of the reasons why there are doubts about the concept of a nonexistent object is this: to be able to truly claim of an object that it doesn't exist, it seems that one has to presuppose that it exists, for doesn't a thing have to exist if we are to make a true claim about it?

Below, we're going to see what can happen when this idea turns up in fiction.

Contrasts: Nonexistence, otherness and Posthumanism

The human encounter with nonexistence is probably the most extravagant event that anyone might imagine ever. So much so, that it is actually unconceivable – precisely because it is a non-event, a void event: in order to "experience" the nonexistence it is necessary to stop being. As stated above, thinking about nonexistence leads to paradoxes we cannot fully solve. Yet, we humans know very well that death does exist: it is what makes us cease to exist, *stop being*.

Earlier we referred to the esthetic astonishment that ensues when, in our role as readers, we come across notions such as nonexistence, nothingness, non-being, etc. This effect makes sense when (as it happens in these texts by Lem and Calvino) the nonexistence is introduced, within a fiction, in an environment of existence. This kind of astonishment is recurring among Stanislaw Lem's readers; and if we think about a Lemian corpus of literary negativities, we could actually mention several texts where at least one of his ideas plays a relevant role either in the discourse or in the fiction. To begin with, the short stories "How The World Was Saved" and "Do You Exist, Mr. Johns?". Moreover, the collection of comments about nonexistent books in *A Perfect Vacuum* (with the particularly remarkable "Rien du tout, ou la consequence"). And also, the novel *Solaris* could be part of this list (which is not comprehensive), as Harey's bod) seems to be "made of nothing" (99). With respect to Italo

Calvino, we could include here his short story "Nothing and Not Much".

It therefore comes as no surprise that the literary works by these two writers show a clear orientation towards some aspects of what we've called the "negative conceptual cluster". Fredric Jameson refers to the "implacable negative and skeptical position" (107) of Lem's most important novels, while Thomas Grob states that "Nothingness, emptiness, and also negation are among his most perennial motifs and approaches" (42). As regards Calvino, Dani Cavallaro claims that his most important books are inspired in topics related to "lack, non-existence and invisibility" (90).

In "The Third Sally" and in *The Nonexistent Knight* the astonishment stems mostly from the way in which fiction, as a potential resource of language, is used to make us imagine creatures, objects and places that seem to contradict a basic rule of literary representation: some nonexistent characters are interacting with other characters that do exist.

Let us analyze this incongruence more in detail. In the short story "The Third Sally, or the Dragons of Probability", the nonexistent condition of the dragons does not prevent science from studying them (85-7) or villages from being struck by them (87). It does not prevent either some unscrupulous character by the name of Basiliscus from bribing the kings with the pretense of negotiating the elimination of the ferocious attackers in exchange of a far too high compensation (88), perhaps due to a device quite similar to the "probability amplifier" previously invented by Trurl (86). Effectively, the dragons against which Trurl and Klapaucius are fighting are partly a consequence of Trurl's own cravings for experimentation and knowledge.

How can we explain that the problems stemming from the dragons are real in the fictional world, despite the fact that in that same fictional world "everyone knows that dragons don't exist" ("Third Sally" 85)? As outlined there, it can happen because these monsters have "an existence quite different from that of ordinary cupboards, tables and chairs; for dragons are distinguished by their probability rather than by their actuality" (86). Then, it means they are not absolutely nonexistent creatures –their existence can be measured with numbers, according to a coding system which, apparently, gives a 10/10 to complete existence and 0/10 to total lack of existence (85, 97).

Separately, in the novel *The Nonexistent Knight*, the above-mentioned property of the knight is underlined at the very beginning. When Agilulf answers Charlemagne's question about why he does not show his face, the knight excuses himself: "Sire, because I do not exist!" (6). During their conversation, Charlemagne includes several references to the nonexistence of his interlocutor, connecting them to specific activities or features ("well said, that is how one does one's duty" (…) "for someone who doesn't exist, you seem in fine form!") (7) as if, ultimately, he couldn't find too many reasons to be impressed, as evidenced by his short-lived astonishment.

Agilulf, with a continuous consciousness and an indivisible identity, exercises his nonexistence with self-determination and responsibility (Calvino 8), even contemptuous of the human race (56-57); his arrogance, however, does not absolve him from frustration and rage (13), of from once even having "a disagreeable feeling resembling envy" (10-11). Something that might well be a special intensity of his own consciousness makes him suffer terribly from an everlasting insomnia (10-11). In *The Nonexistent Knight*, his nonexistence goes in hand with a kind of deformed perfection, combining the isolation of some exaggerated human features with the lack of other essential features. In these as well as in many other cases, the adjective "nonexistent", applied to Agilulf, is connected with other traits that are played out in the world of the narrative: properties united into a character that is a combination of incompatible attributes.

Therefore, the first distinction that can be established between the nonexistence in Lem's short-story and the nonexistence in Calvino's novel is that Agilulf exercises or suffers from a sort of homogeneous nonexistence, complete, permanent, solid and steady, while the dragons faced by Trurl and Klapaucius express theirs partially, in a fragmented, variable, multiple and rather chaotic way.

Another key difference between both texts is the fact that Agilulf reunites his nonexistence and a hybrid between his human and his inhuman condition, while the nonexistence in "Third Sally" is completely disconnected from the humanoid characters (robots Trurl and Klapaucius) and just stays with the dragons, which at the same time embody the creative power of science and what we would call the simultaneous resurrection and death of legends. The dragons of probability are product of a scientific invention that bring monsters to reality (of the fictional world), monsters which only superstitious people believe in ("Third Sally" 91).

Back to the already mentioned incongruence, how can we accept that a few nonexistent characters (from those fiction worlds) show up before other characters who do exist (in those very same fiction worlds)? In a work of fiction, characters and objects appear as a representation of concrete or abstract entities which can or cannot exist in the real world. If there is an imaginary object in a fiction text, this can or cannot be acknowledged as existing in that world (fictitious) by other creatures, that is to say, by the characters. But if a creature whose nonexistence is known by those characters shows up in such fiction world, the reader may choose to call this detail into question. If it is nonexistent in the fiction, how can it possibly interact with the objects and creatures of that world? Something curious happens when, sooner or later, we remember that actually Agilulf and the dragons of probability are nonexistent creatures, even for us (I mean, in our real world). What we can do then is to acknowledge that this kind of literary nonexistence would be a metaleptic irruption of the real world into the fiction; if this is the case, the nonexistence in these stories replicates with striking fidelity — and quite consistently — a very specific aspect of our real world (namely: the total absence of Agilulf and the dragons of probability here too).

In the event that, such as we have guessed, "The Third Sally" and *The Nonexistent Knight* express the fading of some traditional assumptions about humanity and the objects of cultural or scientific knowledge in the aftermath of the social and technological transformations, it would be interesting to point out that these visions are depicted in the fiction (like heroic characters who do not exist or dragons who move about probabilistically between the nonexistence and the existence) through the implementation of elements belonging to the non-human and the inhuman, the superhuman or the infrahuman. This nonexistence would actually be a sign of transformation, a process that would turn the new postmodern subject (individualist, perfectionist, alienated -almost automatic), wandering around the world as if removed from its own era (Agilulf), into something unrecognizable even for humanity. Likewise, this process would also turn all the set of long-held traditions (such as legends, myths –the dragons), reappearing under the new monstrosity granted by the power of knowledge and the control of the matter, into something strange to us, unfamiliar. In this sense, if this transformation implies ceasing to exist as entity A in order to start existing as entity B (thus turning into the Other), then the idea of nonexistence might lose some of its illogical or extravagant shades and become something totally serious to us.

Works Cited

Baldi, Elio. "Science Fiction and the Canon: the Case of Italo Calvino". AAIS Conference, Universität Zürich, May 23-25, 2014.

Bakaoukas, Michael D. "Nonexistence. A comparative-historical analysis of the problem of nonbeing". *E-Logos. Electronic Journal for Philosophy*, Feb. 2014. https://e-logos.vse.cz/artkey/elg-201401-0004.php

Barnouw, Dagmar. "Science Fiction as a Model for Probabilistic Worlds: Stanislaw Lem's Fantastic Empiricism". *Science Fiction Studies*, Vol. 6, No. 2, Jul. 1979, pp 153-163.

Barrow, John D. *The Book of Nothing. Vacuums, Voids, and the Latest Ideas About the Origins of the Universe.* Vintage Books, 2000.

Calvino, Italo. *The Nonexistent Knight and the Cloven Viscount.* Translated by Archibald Colquhoun. Harcourt Brace, 1977, pp 3-141.

Cavallaro, Dani. *The Mind of Italo Calvino. A Critical Exploration of His Thoughts and Writings.* McFarland & Company, Inc., Publishers, 2010.

Crosby, Donald A. *Specter of the Absurd. Sources and Criticisms of Modern Nihilism.* State University of New York, 1988.

Dragonetti, Carmen and Fernando Tola. Introduction: "An Indian Philosophy of Universal Contingency: Nagarjuna's School". *On Voidness. A Study on Buddhist Nihilism*. Motilal Banarsidass Publishers Private Limited, 1995, pp xiii-xxxv.

Déprez, Viviane and M. Teresa Espinal. "Introduction: Negation in Language and Beyond". *The Oxford Handbook of Negation*. Edited by Viviane Déprez and M. Teresa Espinal. Oxford University Press, 2020, pp 1-3. https://www.oxfordhandbooks.com/view/10.1093/oxfordhb/9780198830528.001.0001/oxfordhb-9780198830528-miscMatter-10

Ducrot, Oswald and Tzvetan Todorov. *Encyclopedic Dictionary of the Sciences of Language*. Johns Hopkins University Press, 1983.

Everett, Anthony. The Nonexistent. Oxford University Press, 2013.

Fatone, Vicente. *The Philosophy of Nagarjuna*. Translated by K. D. Prithipaul. Motilal Banarsidass Publishers, Pvt. Ltd, 1981.

Freedman, Carl. *Critical Theory and Science Fiction*. Wesleyan University Press, 2000.

Gomel, Elana. *Science Fiction, Alien Encounters, and the Ethics of Posthumanism*. Palgrave Macmillan, 2014.

Grob, Thomas. Chapter 5 "Into the Void: Philosophical Fantasy and Fantastic Philosophy in the Works of Stanislaw Lem and the Strugatskii Brothers". *Soviet Space Culture. Cosmic Enthusiasm in Socialist Societies*, edited by Eva Maurer, Julia Richers, Monica Rüthers, and Carmen Scheide. Palgrave Macmillan, 2011, pp. 42-56.

Hom, Laurence R. *A Natural History of Negation*.CSLI Publications, 2001.

Hume, Kathryn. "Kathryn Hume on the Novel's Ending". *Bloom's Major Short Story Writers: Italo Calvino*, edited by Harold Bloom. Chelsea House Publishers, 2002, pp 50-52.

Keller, Lech. *Visions of the Future in the Writings of Stanislaw Lem. Volume II: Bibliography*. Thesis. Monash University, 2010.

Jameson, Fredric. *The Desire Called Utopia and Other Science Fictions*. Verso, 2005.

Lem, Stanislaw. "An Interview with Stanislaw Lem", by Wojciech Orlinski. 1996. https://web.archive.org/web/19990224002808/http://www.geocities.com/CapitolHill/2594/lem.html

------. "The Third Sally or the Dragons of Probability". *The Cyberiad. Fables for the Cybernetic Age*, 1974. Translated by Michael Kandel. Harcourt Inc., 1985, pp 85-102.

––––––. *Solaris*, 1987. Translated by Joanna Kilmartin and Steve Cox. Harcourt Inc., 2002.

Lyons, John. *Linguistic Semantics. An Introduction*, 1995. Cambridge University Press, 2005.

McLaughlin, Martin. *Italo Calvino*. Edinburgh University Press, 1998.

Ogden, C. K. and I. A. Richards. *The Meaning of Meaning*. Harcourt, Brace & World, 1923.

Reicher, Maria. "Nonexistent Objects". *The Stanford Encyclopedia of Philosophy*, edited by Edward N. Zalta, 2014, https://plato.stanford.edu/archives/sum2014/entries/nonexistent-objects/

Suvin, Darko. "To Remember Stanislaw Lem". *Extrapolation*, Vol. 47, No. 1, 2006, pp 30-34.

–––––––. "Lem, Stanislaw". *The Encyclopedia of Science Fiction*, 1979, edited by John Clute and Peter Nichols. St. Martin's Press, 1993, pp 710-712.

Swirski, Peter. "The Man Behind the Giant". *The Art and Science of Stanislaw Lem*, edited by Peter Swirski. McGill-Queen's University Press, 2006, pp 3-12.

–––––––. *Stanislaw Lem, Philosopher of the Future*. Liverpool University Press, 2015.

Weiss, Beno. *Understanding Italo Calvino*. University of South Carolina Press, 1993.

Part 3.
Fiction as Science

Air Cows

A Homage to Stanislaw Lem

Neil A. Hogan

The hallway to Professor Henryka Solon's office was hidden between cracked walls and broken masonry, far inside the bomb-damaged research institute. Next to the dusty blanket that hung down over the barely concealed entrance sat a split wooden sign. Politechnika Krakowska im. Stapledon. With so much of the institute destroyed at the end of the war I was surprised my friend had decided to return to her research here.

Behind the blanket things weren't much better. Dripping pipes, cracked walls and a scattering of chunks of cement. Particles of plaster showered on me as I navigated the dangers of the floor towards the peeling wooden door of her office, left invitingly ajar. I pushed it open with an audible screech and looked for her inside.

The only light was feeble, reflected as it were from white walls outside to a dusty window in shade. I could vaguely make out dull shapes inside her office. I felt around for a switch and a tiny lamp sparked on the ceiling, the filament slowly growing brighter. The place smelt of cigarettes and gunpowder. It was then that I was sure. This was another building vacated by the gestapo at the end of the war, but one that had gone unnoticed. Had my friend somehow covered it up? It wouldn't be long before restoration got to this part of Krakow. The government was hell bent on stimulating the economy. Perhaps that was why this meeting was urgent. She was running out of time.

I collapsed into the nearest worn leather chair, relieved to be away from the beating ultraviolet of the sun and dragged an old spotted handkerchief from my trousers' left pocket. The cloth came away from my forehead wet and dark with sweat and dust. I had no doubt the temperature must be higher than the usual twenty-five degrees in July. Perhaps the endless chunks of cement in the area were increasing the heat.

I checked my windup wristwatch. Eleven o'clock. My friend should be here already. Where was she? Perhaps she'd finally given up on her need for punctuality. Then again, perhaps something else had happened. Even though it had been over three years ago, the war was still fresh in my mind, and my fears sometimes ballooned beyond what they should. I clenched my fist, struggling to change my thoughts to being more positive.

Solon, a Doctor of Physics, had requested my appearance with some urgency. A torn piece of paper with a barely legible scrawl had been hastily stuffed into my letter box. It didn't say much. An address, directions, and a time, along with an almost concerning line of desperation. "Dear Doctor Thomasz Lehrman. I need your expertise. Details on the other side. It may be a matter of life and death." Of course, I would never refuse a friend's request for help. However, I had no idea why Solon would request me, specifically. Besides which, she wasn't that close a friend. We had imbibed at a temporary bar called the Fish Out of Water, not long after the war, speaking about the futility of existence and whether humanity was ready for contact with outside intelligences. Other than that, and a few letters over the years, we haven't had much to do with each other.

After resting for a minute, my concern for Solon growing, I got out of the leather chair, now embarrassingly sticky with my sweat, and began to walk around the room. The bulb had fully lit, and I could now see the eclectic collection more clearly. Out of politeness, as though in a museum or library, I kept both hands behind my back, not wanting to give the impression of snooping. I was curious about the objects on display but had no intention of invading Solon's privacy. Admittedly, I knew it was a fine line I frequently trod. As a fill-in teacher at Jagiellonian University, it was expected that I would be interested in almost everything. I felt it a duty, and, if truth be told, I did it in honor of the late Professor Mieczyslaw Malecki. If Malecki hadn't protected my teaching during the occupation, I doubt I'd be here. I would learn and teach whatever I could, though his favorite discipline of linguistics was still not my strong suit.

I was surprised to find that Solon had collected quite a library. Her obsession with quantum physics and fascination with the concept of Einstein-Rosen bridges, not to mention her ability to speak three languages, meant there were titles in Polish, German and English. I was especially impressed by her ownership of a rare copy of Physikalischen Prinzipien der Quantentheorie by Werner Heisenberg, along with a copy of the later unabridged English release -The Physical Principles of the Quantum Theory. Sitting laconically next to it was an even lesser known title Creating Exotic Matter: Theories and Hypotheses by Lien A. Nagoh.

I looked about, confirming that she was still not

approaching the office, then pulled Nagoh's title from the shelf and leafed through it quickly. A contents page with barely comprehensible titles, an author's note confirming that much within was conjecture, with reference to recent research by Doctors Hendrik Casimir and Dirk Polder, then printed plates of his own experiments' notes. He indicated specific geometries could be necessary to enable traversable wormholes that rely on tiny amounts of exotic matter. I turned to the first chapter, Rectangular Prismic Constant Null Energy Condition Violations in Symmetry and briefly scanned the dense text. Without aplomb, his first line was 'Negative energy that repels rather than attracts can create an opposite curve preventing a wormhole throat from pulling in on itself, given symmetrical conditions and a constant energy density.' Further pages revealed he had tested, mathematically, each of the exotic particles currently theorized, all the way to photonic Rydberg atoms. Unfortunately, his final chapter was inconclusive, lamenting that technology did not yet exist for any of his theoretical experiments to be proven. I replaced the book carefully and returned my hands to being innocently behind my back.

Of the shelves of books lining the walls, some were in some semblance of order, some were stacked haphazardly with multiple page corners folded, fattening the volumes and threatening to destabilize the off-center pile. Near the floor sat a wastepaper bin overflowing with yellowing American novels. No doubt Solon had read them for inspiration about wormholes and discarded them when the science wasn't rigorous. Or perhaps they contained too many romances–one of her pet hates.

On the wall, next to the back window, was a framed

faded letter from the institute confirming that they'd nominated Solon for a Nobel prize in physics. I knew she had lost to Isidor Rabi's work on recording the magnetic properties of atomic nuclei, yet she wasn't bitter, stating that Rabi's research was more deserving. I believe this loss a few years ago forced her to work even harder. Another scientist bitten by the Nobel bug.

Had she had a breakthrough? Had she been able to find a place in the universe where the reality of space was thinner? As long as I had known her, she had been obsessed with the idea of opening a hole between points in space. And now, with Krakow reconstruction forces coming ever closer, her laboratory would be rebuilt, delaying her papers.

Whatever it was, she must have discovered something big to call on me so suddenly. Was there something here that could give me a clue?

On a side table sat a magnetophone in mid repair, its innards and magnetic tape spooling around it. Next to it were several reels with simple notes on steel holders. Activation. Analysis. Attempt.

As tempting as playing the reels would be, I felt I had no time to repair the player, so I continued my journey around the collection, almost stumbling over an empty bottle of Spatlese that hadn't been properly discarded, its sticky wine staining the dusty brown carpet. On a shelf above it were several 78rpm phonograph records sitting at a forty-five-degree angle, and a record player leaning gingerly on its side, a thin layer of dust evident. I checked the titles and was surprised to find only English. I Don't Want to Set the World on Fire by the Ink Spots, Star Dust by Artie Shaw, As Time Goes By by Dooley Wilson, and others. I guessed Solon would play these when she had guests. Though, judging by the wine glasses with red spots on the next shelf I was perturbed she had invited them here. Surely this place was still off limits?

In my ruminations, I didn't realize time had moved so quickly. My watch already showed it was quarter after eleven, and yet Solon still hadn't returned for our meeting. I briefly entertained the idea that perhaps the letter was a joke. Then again, it could very well be something worse. Anything could have happened to her since I saw her last. But as one of the last of my friends, I had to give her the benefit of the doubt.

I turned to the table. Solid, mahogany, the desk was strewn with several folders. Numbers, symbols, and equations had been hastily scrawled on their surfaces. Beside them sat a dirty tea mug, stained from multiple uses without cleaning. I frowned at this. Something was wrong, but I couldn't quite work it out. I scanned the room again. The chair was not sitting straight near the table. The folders weren't organized in a pile. Books and other paraphernalia were at various angles.

Then I remembered. She was a perfectionist. I knew everything here belonged to her, but nothing was organized as she would organize it. Had she left and someone had taken her place? Or could the mess indicate the state of Solon's mind, now? For a moment, my breath caught. Had she broken down? Was that the cause of the note? A madwoman's last gasp?

Then I saw it. A book poking out of the collection of folders. The red fabric cover and gold lettering were unmistakable. I took two strides across to the table and dragged the hardback from the folder it was wedged in, staring at it, unbelievingly, my face tightening in anger.

Mein Kampf, by Adolf Hitler.

A noise like the striking of a steel-capped shoe on tile sounded behind me and I turned angrily, thrusting the book under Solon's nose, all thoughts of greetings and politeness forgotten. "What's the meaning of this, Henryka?"

Unfazed, Solon stared me down, her thin, grey eyebrows peering over bifocals. "How dare you assume, Thomasz. Have you been caught up in the witch hunting already? Besides the fact that I have yet to give you permission to look through my desk, you're not even allowing me the benefit of the doubt?" She frowned. "I hope you're not as quick to judge the case I have for you."

Shocked at my own behavior and mortified that I might have offended her, I stepped back and lowered the book. "I'm sorry." I took a couple of deep breaths to calm myself, marveling at the slight smile that played over her face. "Surely you're more than angry with me?"

"Of course not, by dear Thomasz. But you saved me having to test whether you're a sympathizer!" Then she gave one of her polite coughs and took the book from me, placing it back in the folder. "If you must know, I took it from one of the lockers upstairs next to Doctor Gottfried Meier's room. Left by the Nazis I expect. I'm sure there are more. Like Catholics leaving bibles everywhere hoping to inspire people to their cause."

"I'm sorry," I muttered again. "Not the best start, then."

"It's about to get much worse, I assure you." She pushed aside some of the folders and retrieved another. Plain manila coloring with no marks on it. Conspicuous by its unsullied look. She held it out to me, then looked me in the eye. "Oh, please sit down. You're making me nervous."

I smiled and sat thankfully, struggling to push my recent behavior from my mind. I was here for her. I gingerly took the folder and flipped to the first few pieces of yellowing paper.

"Did you find this place alright?" She asked, deliberately moving on from the past few moments.

"After skirting a few roped-off areas, I was inspired to follow a clear path that led me straight here."

"Good. Good. Yes. We must follow our inspirations. It can lead to surprising things."

The papers seemed unintelligible. Higher level calculations using equations challenging physics. "I think this is a bit over my head, Henny. What am I looking at?"

"Everything I could find on Gottfried's research, before he went, well, you'll see. I have not experienced the same effect that my colleague has, after seeing the beings, and that is why I have brought you here."

"Beings?"

My mind froze for a moment. I had been completely focused on space bridges, forgetting the whole point of creating one. Had she met extra-terrestrial biological entities? "I'm sorry, but I think I missed something."

"Contact has been, well, attempted," said Solon. "But we have no way of understanding them."

"You opened a portal? How?" I suddenly felt like the situation was running away from me.

"All in good time. Firstly, Gottfried is now beyond me, I feel. I need your help with him."

I frowned. "Look. I think I need more detail. I mean,

obviously you've called me in to be a psychologist, and I've studied how to help those suffering from the vapors. But if it's because he's seen something not of this Earth…"

Solon nodded.

"My studies in psychology were just an idle curiosity," I continued. "His condition is most likely to be beyond what I know."

"And yet, you still had a paper in a peer-reviewed journal. Psychological Nomenclature Volume 47, as I recall."

I nodded, dumbly. Not my greatest work.

"Before the war, you proposed the idea that women love circular things yet are sexually attracted to rectangular shapes and that men love rectangular things yet are sexually attracted to circular shapes. You even came to the attention of Freud, as I recall."

"It was just an observation," I protested, meekly, secretly enjoying the praise. "I didn't take into account those who were attracted to the same sex or no sex, so the report was incomplete."

"Even so, those of us in the physics community were impressed. The idea that geometry and sexuality could somehow be linked. It was why we got talking at the bar those years ago. And now I need that same thinking here."

"But Henny! Beings from another world! Before I see Gottfried, I just have to see these creatures for myself!"

Solon sighed. "I've been studying them for more than a month now so the shine has gone off them, you could say. Of course, you should be excited. As we've discussed over copious glasses of syrah, the immensity of the universe doesn't preclude the existence of other intelligent life. We simply expected them to be there, and they were."

For many years, I'd had an interest in space fiction, in particular the concept of meeting something non anthropomorphic and more intelligent. My interest was first piqued with the translated works of H.G. Wells, Jules Verne, and Mary Shelley before exploring harder-to-find works, in Poland at any rate, in such English language magazines as Astonishing Stories. I believe I read up until volume 4 issue 4 but haven't been able to find the next issue yet. I also very much enjoyed a serialized story in Nowy Świat Przygód called Człowiek z Marsa by a new author whose name didn't immediately come to mind. In any case, my simultaneous fascination with astronomy has meant that I've never believed that this is the only star with planets around it. There had to be others.

Solon sat back in her own burgundy chair and steepled her fingers, allowing me a moment. I'd only ever seen her in her professor clothes. To see her here, wearing a short-sleeved shirt and overalls, seemed out of place. It might have even been the first time I've ever seen her arms. She had truly relaxed in the past few years.

My elation at the possibility that humanity was not alone made me almost forget the book that had been hidden from view. Still, it was a sore point that would never go away. It was sheer luck that I was still alive, thanks to being stuck in an elevator and never attending the seminar organized for over 200 academics. The nazis had quickly rounded them up and either arrested and jailed or executed them, depending on their importance. I briefly wondered how Solon had avoided that too but then remembered not every academic had been invited.

But there was an increasing churning in the pit of my

stomach. Something was wrong. It wasn't just the disorganization in the office. Was it something about Solon herself? I hadn't seen her in years, but I hadn't expected her to have so much grey hair in her early fifties, and so many lines. She was even stooped. Do women in their early fifties stoop? Age spots, skin that once held muscle now hanging in thick flaps of fat under her upper arms…

She suddenly jumped up out of the chair, belying her fragile appearance, and grabbed her cane. Then, as though suddenly realizing she was older than she felt, gasped and supported herself before moving forward. Whatever had happened to her had been recent, and she had yet to adjust to it. She stopped again, waving her hand in front of her face, and I could see her skin reddening. "My apologies," she muttered. "I don't know what is coming over me these days. Getting these hot flushes all of a sudden. Old age is creeping up on me."

I followed Solon as she carefully made her way out of the office and turned left into a darkened corridor that looked more like a mining tunnel. Pieces of wood held up cracking plaster, and broken pipes and bits of timber littered the cement flooring. I half expected to see carts on tracks waiting for chunks of rock replete with crystals, or striations of gold and silver to be piled into them. But the swaying and tapping of the cane from my old friend slowly pulling herself along, concerned me greatly.

My father had worked the farms last century and had made it, fit and active, to the ripe old age of 92, dying before the war began. Yet, Solon looked like she would die at any moment.

"Are you ill?" I asked, as she shuffled further along.

"What?" she answered gruffly. "No! Of course not!"

"You didn't have that cane before. I don't remember you ever having any grey either."

"My frailty is just your perception. It's all about this." Solon tapped her leg, looking meaningfully back. "I've got an overabundance of uric crystals collecting in my joints. You might know it as gout and arthritis. Seems to be spreading. Well, the swelling is, at any rate. An annoyance, only."

She stopped and pointed her cane at me. "I need you to help me with Gottfried, but also because, soon I can't be here. An operation. You could mind the place for me, if the door interests you."

My interest was indeed piqued, especially as the offhandedly mentioned door must be her very own Einstein-Rosen Bridge. But gout? A rich person's disease. As far as I knew, Solon continued to live the modest life of a scientist. "And your drinking?"

"How is that related?"

"Well, it's been suggested that alcohol…and meat…"

"I barely touch alcohol. A glass of red wine or two at the end of a hard day."

"Is every day a hard day?"

"And what, pray tell, are you insinuating? Aren't you a year older? I'm not looking for a father figure!"

I could hear a slight smile in the answer and gave a polite laugh. Perhaps I was worrying too much. Of course, she was her own person. I had no right or responsibility to consider myself the arbiter of her health. Years of being concerned for young adults has brought out the father in me. This briefly encouraged a bout of maudlin self-pity, and regretful thoughts about my wife not having been able to have children due to endometrial adenomas. I let out a hard breath. This was supposed to be a light conversation, yet I was making it heavier. Was there something in the air, or lack of something, that was bringing this negativity on me? Was it the crushing evidence of the war that was constantly on my periphery?

At that moment Solon swung her cane back in front of me like a conductor, then pointed at a wooden wall panel. She gave it two sharp taps, then stood back. It sprang up to reveal an ancient elevator, two manual wire doors protecting its occupants from certain death. "We're going down to the basement."

I stepped back, terror flooding my mind, the walls around me feeling just that bit closer. "In an…in an elevator? Aren't there stairs anywhere? How big is this place that it needs one of those?"

Solon stared at me, piercing blue eyes searching my whiter face. "I don't remember you being claustrophobic."

"Not exactly. I was trapped in one for several hours during the war. I thought I was going to die there. It comes back to me regularly. Nightmares."

Solon bared her grey teeth in a grin. "Excellent. You're here with an understanding friend. It's another opportunity to fight it!" She turned back and struggled briefly with the grid of metal strips that made up the first door before it relented and, screeching, let itself be pushed to the right. She then pulled the much easier inner door across with a well-oiled clang and pointed at the dark and foreboding interior, lit sullenly by one yellow light from the well.

I could feel a sheen of sweat developing on my

forehead, and my armpits had decided to open the floodgates. If I had not have been wearing a suit jacket, Solon would have seen the rapidly spreading patches down my sides. I held up my hands in defeat. "You're right. It's childish," I said, sounding like I had more confidence than I could muster. I was determined to cross the gap between the doors when my body simply stopped me. It was as though thick ropes, like those used to anchor boats at wharves, had been wrapped around my knees. My legs simply couldn't move. The fear had gripped my body tightly, freezing me in place. I blinked and fought myself muttering the best swear words Polish had to offer.

"Yes, you need to break the disempowering feeling. Anger can do that. Swear some more! With gusto!" Solon was nodding encouragingly at me. I raised an eyebrow at her, thinking, who was being the father figure now? More to the point, who had studied psychology more?

Even so, the distraction worked, and the first leg moved, and then the second, carrying me to the door.

"See," said Solon, distracting me further with a louder and confident voice. "Nothing to it!" She patted me on the back and in surprise I stumbled further into the elevator. Solon quickly dragged both doors shut and pulled down on a lever.

I spun, fear rising in my throat as the metal gears engaged and, with a clack that sounded like a pistol shot, the elevator shuddered and screeched into the depths below.

I saw Solon briefly frown at the sound, but she shrugged it off and just said "Old lift." She checked that everything was moving smoothly then turned back to me. "It's a short ride but I best get your mind off it and inform you of the entities."

I watched the cement walls slide slowly past, their surfaces getting older and darker. More pockmarks appeared and even a kind of powdery residue began to encroach on the surface. This was unusual, as my understanding was that concrete can last for centuries without changing much at all. Perhaps the institute was built over older buildings, maybe even structures left over from Roman times.

"I saw you looking at my tapes as I rounded the corner," she continued. "They're not that compelling, so you've saved yourself some time. Lots of 'at a quarter to four' this happened and 'at half past twelve' that happened."

I was holding one of the support bars, my knuckles white. I could barely hear her, desperate to get out, fighting my fear and wanting it to be over. I gritted my teeth and forced a smile. Solon pretended not to notice my discomfort, out of politeness, I gathered.

"Though, the third tape might be more of interest. It covers the activation of the Einstein-Rosen bridge, the analysis of the microwave radiation it exuded, and the discovery of the Other."

I nodded automatically. Then, much to my relief, the cage landed with a thud, jerk and screech of brakes. The wall in front lifted open and bright red light flooded the elevator. I breathed a sigh of relief and waited for Solon to open the door. She turned to me with a surprised look on her face and said. "Oh, no. I forgot something. We'll have to go back."

I stared at her in horror, then she cackled, turned back and pulled open the door.

"A little joke of mine," she said over her shoulder. "I'd

rather you be angry at me than terrified of a perfectly safe platform, with multiple brake stops, operated with electric pulleys on reserve power."

Irrationally, or perhaps rationally, I wanted to scream at her. I took a deep breath, expelled hard, then followed quickly behind.

The concrete room was lit red, with what looked to be black scorch marks in a rectangular shape near the center, as though someone had taken a blow torch to the area. A space had been cleared in roughly the same place and I realized with some concern that the blackened area spread almost evenly from a terrifying burning door on the right.

"Welcome to the hell door," said Solon, flicking a hand in its direction with a flourish. She then eagerly went over to it, possibly her thoughts of Gottfried and even her cane forgotten. It clattered to the floor just outside the elevator. She turned back to me for a moment. "Sorry that I was late. I just came back from there." She pointed at the door.

The 'hell door' had a grid of wires across it. I walked closer, then felt my face burning and stepped back. "Radiation?"

"Microwave radiation. Falls off outside three meters. Limited effects if you stand on the other side of the burn. The faraday cage is keeping most of it in."

I viewed the contraption from a safer distance. The door was ringed with coils of copper, tied with black tape. Cables ran from these into a petrol generator, next to which were buckets of fuel. I grimaced at the carelessness, but pressed Solon for more information. "The generator is off. How is it working?"

"It's not. Well, not exactly."

I pointed at the door. "Well, obviously, it is!"

"Yes, but not on this side. Once established, it became self-sustaining. I still haven't worked out why. But I kept the generator here, just in case. If it ever turns off when one of us is on the other side, we're ready to turn it on again. However, it's been three weeks, and it's unlikely Gottfried would have the mental acuity to turn it on again, now."

I pulled at my sticky shirt. "It must be over thirty degrees Celsius in here. Is there a danger to Krakow?"

"The microwaves haven't spread beyond this room as far as I can detect. We could probably just collapse the building over it and, without the door utilizing the stable electromagnetic coils around it, it would cease to be."

"Theoretically. Wasn't it that the gestapo tried to destroy the institute and failed?"

"Oh, they destroyed a lot. Half of the building is unusable. But the grenade they had here needed to be manually set off, and it wasn't."

Staring at the heat field of the door, seeing the fluctuations in the red light, feeling my hands burning even though I considered myself to be far enough away, I was suddenly struck by the inanity of it. Solon had opened a portal to another world with no control, and had left it connected. While the grill door would have stopped anything coming through, the fact that it was there meant that someone or something on the other side could break through it sometime in the future. It wasn't beyond the realms of possibility. And if she had somehow connected to a world with beings worse than the Nazis' then it was the end for humanity as we knew it.

"Henryka. Your scrawled note had me starting to

wonder about your sanity. Now I'm sure. Close this down. Blow it up. What if intelligences came through and decided they liked what they saw? You'd be replacing one invasion with another."

"There's nothing dangerous on the other side, I assure you."

"You've connected to a whole planet! Have you explored the entire planet in just a few weeks?"

"No. I haven't left the plateau. Look. Tomasz. You just have to trust me on this. Seriously, you're a multidisciplinary teacher. Where is that famous open mind of yours?"

I was about to remonstrate further but it was another valid point, though I suspected I was about to be sacrificed by my own hubris. I sighed and continued listening.

"Just your opinion on something is needed. Nothing more. I'll take you through the portal and show you the other side. If, after that, you want nothing to do with this, you can turn your back and leave me to deal with Gottfried. But, if you want to help, I'd be grateful if you could stay."

I looked into Solon's eyes, now imploring, and grunted. "Fine." Then the full force of what she had said hit me. "We're going through that?"

She grinned and pointed at three hazardous material suits lying across a nearby table. She picked one up. I could see scuff marks on the material, and smears on the glass. Second hand. I grimaced.

"The microwave radiation is only damaging at the edge of the doorway. Once inside, it surrounds us briefly in a protective toroidal shape. Our momentum then takes us through the other side. Well, it's such a short trip you wouldn't notice it, but make sure you move quickly, otherwise you might be stuck."

"I'm not sure."

"I've been through at least ten times. Live a little."

"And Gottfried?"

"Once was enough for him."

"Oh, and you don't think my mind might suddenly be affected by whatever is on the other side?"

"No. I do not. Besides, his madness came a few weeks later."

"This does not fill me with confidence."

She pressed the suit into my hands. "It's worth it, I assure you."

I began putting on the suit, while she put on hers, my hands shaking. I pulled the pants up over my trousers and pulled the top part down over my jacket. Then I fitted the rubber helmet with the glass faceplate and filter. I could smell garlic and cabbage coming from the glass. If they'd been cleaned, it wasn't too well. "This won't protect me from radiation."

"No."

"…or viruses."

"Make sure your gloves are secure."

"This is just for chemicals. What chemicals will we encounter?"

"We haven't yet, but it's all we have. If you like, we can shower in them when we return." With that, Solon pulled the door open. Immediately, the cement near my feet began to waver with the intense heat.

"It's about fifty degrees. Imagine you're jumping through a hot shower."

"For God's sake," I said, my fear increasing.

It was then that I noticed the noise. The door had also been preventing sounds from that otherworldly connection. Now I could make out a rending, screeching note as though space itself was being torn. There was also a deep hum underlying everything. The flaming red of the door, now boiling like the surface of the Sun, did not give me any confidence in surviving it safely.

Solon gave me an encouraging nod through her face plate then jumped into the portal and was gone.

For a moment, I stopped, hesitating, looking around the room. The fear of death played through my mind and body. The parallels between this and my imagined nightmares of body furnaces and all the friends and family I'd lost weighed heavily. Like in a dream I reached out and touched the flames.

Then a gloved hand reached through from the other side and pulled me bodily into the burning light.

Moments later, I was stumbling onto hard dirt, bright spots in my vision, coughing at the multiple smells. I sat on my haunches, hands on the ground, getting my breath. The first thing I noticed was a high concentration of methane. I blinked away the burns from my retina and did my best to focus. The environment was blurred, and I grimaced at the thought of having to get stronger glasses.

Solon pulled me up and away from the door, indicating the scorched rectangle in the dirt in front of it. "Safer over here," she said. She could see me blinking, looking down, trying to see. "Your senses need a minute or so to adjust."

Eventually my focus returned, and I was able to see strange yellowish lichen growing on pebble-like rocks on the ground, splashes of spidery white shapes, possibly mold, splayed out from them. Fat purple leaves gripped the soil with what looked like root spikes. Whatever I was looking at I had never seen before. Yet, they could very well be undiscovered plants and molds on Earth. "Photosynthesis?"

Solon helped me to my feet. "You tell me."

As my focus returned, I could see we were on some kind of half plateau, with piles of rocks leading to the start of the incline of a mountain. I looked up but felt a slight tightness in my neck. I also felt my over-the-belt stomach weighing a little more than usual. "Gravity is slightly higher," I said.

"The difference is so small, only scientists would notice the difference," she said, beaming at my awareness.

Then I gasped as the full enormity of what had just occurred hit me. I was no longer wandering a bombed-out institute in the middle of Krakow. I was far beyond all that. Far beyond the limitations of humanity. "Oh. My. God. We're on another planet."

"Freeing, isn't it?" said Solon. "You could stay here and forget everything. Better than retiring."

I looked up and found the star on the edge of the horizon. Very similar to Sol. "Yellow dwarf star?

She nodded.

"Plants also similar to our own. Panspermia?"

"Perhaps over thousands of years. I calculated the positions of the stars with reference to our own and can confirm we're a bit further around the galaxy."

Staring at the doorway across space, I began to understand the implications. "So, thanks to you, space can now be easily navigated. We just need to find where one point in space meets another point. We're no longer trapped here, well, there."

"Like a two-dimensional sheet curled into a three-dimensional tube. Those living on it would have no idea they could simply drill through to the other side."

"And now you have a way to curl a sphere into something in another dimension and join the points together."

Solon nodded. "The Nazis had got close, but they were looking for a way to open one directly to London. It doesn't work that way. The further the distance, the more likely the destination will work. Not only that, we also don't have enough energy on the entire planet to break open a new Einstein-Rosen bridge within the universe. But, if we can find an already existing opening, and just add matter with a negative energy density and a large negative pressure, we can stabilize it."

"How on Earth did you get hold of exotic matter?"

"I created it. You know, one of the reasons I have yet to get the Nobel is because my research has absolutely no use yet. What possible point could creating exotic particles have besides to say you can? But, by using them to open a wormhole, well, genius does spring to mind."

"What's another reason?"

"How many females do you know who've won the Nobel for physics?"

For a moment my mouth opened. It honestly hadn't occurred to me that there could be something to prevent a woman from winning it. "Lots of women have won Nobels but…."

"For peace, literature and chemistry. But for physics?"

I struggled to remember. "Marie Curie!"

"Over forty years ago!" she said bitterly. "Even after a hundred years I'm sure I'll still be able to list the female physics winners on one hand."

I didn't know what to say to that, but I had trouble focusing anyway. We'd just gone through a wormhole. We were on another planet! "Look. Let's talk about that later. I want you to tell me more about this." I pointed at the door. "I guess you tested it with some rats in a cage first. Any changes to them?"

"None whatsoever," she said, brightening again. "They died of natural causes a few weeks later."

"I've read Einstein and Rosen's theory. Taught it, actually. It's difficult to create exotic particles on Earth due to the gravity."

Solon grinned. "Essentially that door consists of a fluidic sheet of compressed particles packed closely together, generating the negative force, but vibrating in a way that they mostly pass through you. You don't have to interact with them."

"Forgive me, my dear Henny, but I'm finding all this difficult to believe. Firstly, your research area in the institute is the only one that is not destroyed. Then, you find experiments from our enemies, that you instantly understand. Not only that, it's something your research needs. Then, in the exact same place, you find a weakness in space in the center of Krakow and you're able to use that to create a wormhole to another world. But, and this is the unbelievable part, you're somehow able to create the matter needed to stabilize it. You jump through the door and survive, then come back and take someone else with you. Do you know how incredible all this sounds?"

"And yet, here we are." She frowned at me. "You can't even believe what you see with your own eyes? You'd make a great judge!" She hmphed. "The gestapo took over my laboratory. I was almost at a breakthrough when they commandeered everything. When they left, of course I returned. They had built on what I had done, then I built on what they had done. It led me to paths I would never have thought of, speeding up the creation of the door, probably by a year or two. Even so, this door wasn't an overnight discovery. It's ten years of painstaking research and experimentation!"

She took a breath and let it out slowly, her glass face plate briefly fogging up. "In any case, I brought you here to satisfy your curiosity about the beings and not only to get you in a position where you might be able to better understand poor Gottfried, but to also to discuss evolution with you." She looked over my shoulder and pointed. "Look, now, and tell me what you think."

I sighed and turned in the direction she was pointing. Far off to the right, beyond the plateau, drifting over a line of grass covered mountains, I could barely see what looked like shadowy bubbles coming closer. Moments later I could make them out and almost fell over in shock. My eyes struggled to understand the creatures. Like a variety of upside-down hot air balloons, they rose and fell slowly, with the air currents. One got closer, and I could see a single dark brown wrinkled extrusion on its surface. As soon as the first creature arrived at the plateau it released gas and lowered itself to the ground. It was then that I saw the mound contained a rudimentary mouth. It opened and released a proboscis-like tongue, then slid it across the lichen, pulling some of it in, leaving a sticky white trail in its wake.

"What do you think of our air cows?" asked Solon.

For a moment I was stunned. The creature continued to lick the lichen with its long pink tongue and then, as though its stomachs had started producing whatever gasses were keeping them airborne, it was dragged back into the sky. More air cows began descending, searching for their own lichen. "They like the lichen-like plants?"

"I think it is all they like. I guess the cyanobacteria create the gas that keeps them airborne. My plan was to capture one, but I need more people and, well, until I've mitigated the risk, I can't."

The softer, more fragile-looking spherical creatures soon gave way to squarer, more solid-looking ones. When the spherical ones had all returned to the sky, the squarer ones dipped down to take their fill, in almost regimented fashion. Were they security guards protecting their queen or were they defensive partners? Then again, the softer ones could very well be males, or they're a different species working together.

The squarer ones soon launched themselves into the air again and headed to the front of the cloud.

"At the risk of anthropomorphizing, are the rounder ones female and the squarer ones male?"

"I believe so. I've started coming here and sitting for a while looking for inspiration. I've sometimes done my best work doing nothing. I guess it was because I was unmoving that they didn't notice me and were more relaxed. It was then that I saw one of the bulls release an extensor that was almost as long as a whale's, then penetrate one of the cows from behind. They stayed together in the air for a while before the bull floated down to sleep."

"And you've tried to communicate with them?"

"I have. I've tried speaking, yelling, sign language, sounds. I've even sat cross-legged over there for an hour, sending out my thoughts, in case they could somehow pick up the electrical signals in my brain. No response. Occasionally, they make a whistling noise when they let excess gas escape, but there are no responses from the others when that happens, so I don't think they have a language. Perhaps they communicate in ways beyond our understanding."

I stared at them further for a moment then turned back to her. "What opinion are you looking for, here?"

Solon pointed. "I've read Darwin's theory of evolution. I've even done some of my own experiments on finches. But you've taught it at university. I want you to tell me, how could something like that evolve?"

I stared at the creatures. Was it the craziness of the morning or was I suffering the effects of the methane? Perhaps I'd hung around university students for too long. But the air cows could only remind me of one thing. "How is it that the first life form humans meet look like floating breasts?"

Solon frowned at my childishness. "Really, Thomasz. It is our distance of perception, only. I was able to get close to one and saw tiny eyes and a mouth on the nipple-shaped mound, and much of the 'mammary' skin has mole-like patches that I think are its way of sensing the environment."

"How do they breed?"

"I have a theory that they're like oversized bacteria.

Certainly, to maintain their gas they would need bacteria to create it. However, none look as though they're going to go through binary fission, there's no ability to lay eggs or have a live birth so, I'm not sure. For all I know, this group might be the final stage, after all the childbearing."

The air cows were continuing their search for pasture, using the methane they expelled to propel them in a new direction. I surmised their anal sphincter must be incredibly advanced for them to have that kind of control.

"So, Thomasz, what do you think? Will you help bring Gottfried back to us and then help with our research on these creatures? He's not in any condition to be seen by anyone publicly, and being a German scientist, he might get caught up in the trials."

My eyes narrowed, in spite of myself. Even light years away from it all, in my head I couldn't resist taking myself back there. "You're protecting him?"

"Gottfriend was a special case. He was working undercover as part of the Red Orchestra German resistance group. It was he who didn't let off the bomb here."

I sighed, then indicated the air cows. "This seems like everything we've ever done on Earth has less relevance. I mean, people fought over land, but you've just proven the universe is full of it and we never need to be territorial again."

"Well, early days for that," said Solon, and she made her way back to the glowing red hole.

"Right." I followed her lead.

I felt the blast of heat as I approached the door, and the glass plate in front of my face instantly became too hot. I pushed through the doorway quickly after Solon, eager to get back to safety, while at the same time keeping my head as far away from the front of my helmet as possible.

I stumbled into the underground room and, when I straightened, I saw that Solon had frozen in front me. For a moment, I wasn't sure what was happening and was about to reach out to touch my friend's shoulder when I began to sense another presence in the room.

Solon raised her arms.

I stepped quickly to my left, fear welling up in me that the Nazis had returned, then raised my arms as well.

Meier had been waiting for us, and was holding a Walther P-38 pistol, directed at Solon's chest.

"My dear Gottfried," began Solon, carefully. "Pray, tell, what is the meaning of this?"

"Henny," I muttered. "I don't think…"

"Shut up," yelled Meier, his strident voice echoing around the chamber. He moved closer to Solon. "It's your fault. You fated us. Now, it's the end of humanity as we know it."

Solon shook her hands in a way that looked like rainwater coming down. Meier frowned. "It's too late. A shower won't do anything. The infection is already here!"

"Henny," I whispered. "What is he talking about? I thought he was on our side!"

"Honestly," Solon muttered back, "I have no idea."

Meier waved the gun around and yelled at us. "Stop speaking in Polish. English from both of you."

"Doctor Meier," I began, in stuttering English. My skill was not yet at the level of linking words, and I just hoped he would understand my 'th' sounds. "It is a pleasure to meet you." I said this in as friendly a way as I could muster. "I've heard so much about you, and I'm here to help. What can we do to make this situation better?"

Meier's gun wavered between us. "Shut it off. Now!"

Solon sighed. "Gottfried. We've been through this. I can't shut it off from this end."

Meier shook his head. "No. You think I'm a child because I can't speak Polish. You've become racist in your old age, Henryka. An entire country with just white people. Your mind has closed."

"I've never, ever made that judgement," said Solon. "I found you hiding here. I've brought you food and drink. I've even organized a stipend. Our relationship is professional, but I really would like you to consider me as a friend."

The P-38 moved from Solon to me, and back again. I'd seen what they could do, but I was sure that my own medical knowledge would patch up some minor wounds. Of course, I also knew a shot to the head, heart, or abdomen was fatal. And, if Meier decided to use the entire magazine…He didn't seem to be aiming it at any specific part of our bodies, so I suspected this was simply an idle threat. Even so, his wavering back and forth and his unfocused look meant I knew it might be difficult to talk him out of it if he did decide to shoot. If I could give him what he wanted, I could take the gun in a moment of weakness. Well, unless Solon had a plan, but she looked as fearful as I had been in the elevator only a few minutes ago.

"Standard issue, I heard," I said, making light conversation. "Quite efficient. Recoil is easy on the wrist. I'd recommend it to my daughters if I had had any."

It seemed like he didn't hear me.

I decided to try a different tact. "Where are my

manners? Doctor Meier. My name is Tomasz Lehrman. Science and social science teacher, though I like to say I'm more of a filler-in-er-er! Professor Solon has told me wonderful things about you."

Tears began streaming down Meier's face. "I'm sorry," he said, choking up, his mind on other things. "I've done the calculations. I know why it remains open. And I know how to close it. Only a human sacrifice will end this hell." Then, as though realizing what he just said, muttered, "Ironic, I think."

With that, Meier fired the pistol. His lack of focus, and the recoil meant his aim was off and the bullet shot through Solon's arm.

Solon cried out and fell to the floor.

I saw my chance and dived at Meier, wrenching the firearm from him.

Meier, his chance lost, his position of power taken away, collapsed onto the blackened floor, sobbing. It was then that I noticed the bulge on the back of his neck. It looked to be some kind of boil or pustule, but it was getting larger before my eyes.

One thing at a time, I thought. I turned back to Solon. Blood had begun dripping out of the upper section of her suit. "What can I do?" I asked, forlornly.

She gripped her arm, swearing. "Jasna cholera! Gowno!" Then she looked at Meier. "Cewi!"

Meier groaned, and I could see that he had been holding on until the last. Whatever disease he had caught was spreading rapidly. His neck had darkened and the skin under his hair had begun swelling. But what could cause such rapid disintegration of human tissue? I carefully turned him over and was surprised to see that his face had now swelled so much his eyes had sunk into the pink flesh. I shuddered. It was like lymphatic filariasis had taken over his head. I had heard of insect infestations in people who had visited sub-Saharan Africa and not taken the proper precautions, but I doubted he'd been outside of Poland for years.

"Too late," I heard him mumble. "Too late."

"What's too late?" I moved closer to hear, believing Meier was beyond help, but to my surprise, he reared up and snatched the pistol from me. For a brief moment he pointed it at me, perhaps to recapture his feeling of power over us, then he slowly turned the pistol on himself.

"Too late, for me," he said. As he pulled the trigger, I realized he had just wanted an audience.

I turned away, avoiding the spurt of blood that shot across the room. I'd seen enough death in my life. It was then that I remembered the gunshot sound while in the elevator. Meier had probably been making sure the gun worked.

Solon groaned. "Too late. I'm always too late. I'm sorry, friend."

I took the gun from Meier's hand again and put it carefully on the table, paying my last respects. "I'm sorry." I turned back to Solon, my sensibilities finally overriding my clinical detachment. A man had just killed himself in front of me, and I might even have had a hand in his demise. I was at a loss as to what to do next.

Solon had regained some of her strength and had stood up, gasping. The blood had stopped dripping from under her protective tunic. "Tissue samples. If he brought something back from the planet, we need to know about it."

"But…" I began. "He brought something back?" I was going to grab her shoulders but remembered her injury, and my arms just dropped impotently. "For God's sake, Henryka. What about us?"

"We went with suits. He did not."

I sighed and let go. It wasn't an answer to my question but for now I didn't want to think about it. "We have to get that wound bandaged first." I pointed at her arm.

Solon showed me her arm through the hole of her suit. All that was left was a bruise. "Went straight through, then healed quickly," she said. "I know what you're thinking. I can't explain it either."

* * *

I stood over the corpse of the late Doctor Gottfried Meier and grimaced at the blackening skin. Whatever he'd been suffering from, death had accelerated it. Or perhaps it was the heat of the room. Rigor mortis had become apparent in his legs while in other parts his bacteria had already started munching away at his innards. I probably had an hour at most.

Solon set up a table with various tools that were close as possible to surgical instruments, but I was more concerned about not only what diseases might present themselves that could be passed onto the living, but how to explain his suicide to the authorities.

A sound of metal scratching wood and I glanced over to see Solon sliding a small microscope towards me. I raised an eyebrow through my helmet glass. "That's all you've got? I'll barely be able to see parasites!"

"Do your best," she said, then backed away and sat to the side of the doorway, watching.

I got to work, taking tissue samples from both clean and swollen parts of Gottfried's body and putting them between glass slides. The microscope's lenses were worse than I thought. Without an internal lamp, I could barely make out the constituents of Gottfried's blood. Plasma, red blood cells, white blood cells, platelets. They were there but, strange. As though they'd been stretched or swollen like the skin holding them. I prepared another slide and got the same result. There also seemed to be a thickening ichor between them, as though an unseen cell was working hard to congeal everything.

"No parasites that I can see."

"The cells, Thomasz." Solon asked, impatiently. "What about the cells?"

"They seem, well, swollen."

"Are they still human?"

I looked up at her. "What?"

"I mean, taking Erwin Schrödinger's idea of an irregular crystal chromosome preserving the genes, have his genes changed in any way?"

"Since when did you study biophysics?"

"Like you, I dabble in everything."

I pushed the microscope aside. "We need something more powerful if you want me to check whether his DNA has changed. A lot more powerful."

"Hypothesize then." She pointed at the body and I was disturbed to see that the bloating of the skin had continued to spread. I stood back from it and watched as Meier's shoulders started to fatten, the smell of decay becoming stronger.

"The bacteria is really enjoying his body," I muttered, bile rising in my throat. "I must admit to being quite disgusted right now. Is there somewhere we can store him? I don't think I'm going to find out anything this way."

"Cold room?"

I found a white furniture sheet and we rolled his body onto it and covered him, then lifted him onto a metal gurney and rolled him into the cold room. I was surprised Solon made no further mention of her bullet wound. Surely there would have been at least some kind of twinge of pain, but she showed nothing.

On a nearby metal shelf, sitting innocuously, was a long tan-colored wooden handle, screwed atop of which was a cylinder. I knew exactly what it was. "Is that entirely safe? There's at least 170g of TNT in there. How did you get an M43?"

Solon sighed. "This Stielhandgranate is the one Gottfried had offered to explode, before hiding out."

I grunted at this revelation. "What do you think he meant by human sacrifice?"

She shrugged. "Madness had got to him, I expect. But we could check his notes. His room is on the first level near the lift. I'm sorry that you didn't have a chance to save him from himself, but perhaps he had been working on a way to save us from ours."

I positioned the gurney securely, taking a last fearful look at the M43, then headed back out of the cold room, Solon shutting it behind me. I checked my watch and was surprised to find it had stopped at a quarter to six. Had it really been that long?

I would check the time when I left and then reset the watch and wind it up again. Until then, I had another challenge to face. The ride back up.

It was then that I noticed something more disturbing than I had thought possible. The suit of Solon's entire leg had swollen, enough that it looked ready to burst. "Henny. I think you need to get that leg checked as soon as possible."

Solon turned to remonstrate with me, then realized her leg was not responding. She stared at it, like observing an experiment. "It's swelling, like Gottfried's head."

My fear of a sudden infection that could kill me overrode my fear of elevators and I raced to the door, pulling back on the grating and the inner door, then diving inside.

Solon struggled to follow me, but I'd already seen enough. I had to quarantine her. "I'm sorry. I'll get help!"

Realizing what I had planned she screamed at me "Don't you dare trap me here!"

I slammed the lever and the elevator slowly climbed with the sound of Solon's cane smacking feebly on the outer gate. I'd gone from being amongst scientists to fighting for my life in a house of horrors. This must have been how Doctor Frankenstein had felt.

It was then that it occurred to me that if both of us had picked up something from that planet, and Solon had become infected even though she had taken the proper precautions, then it could only mean that I had caught it, too. If I go back outside, I might be responsible for killing others.

I gritted my teeth then called down. "I'll find an answer. I'll figure this out. I'm not leaving. I'm going to check for information. Meier's notes. There has to be a solution. Then, I'll join you in quarantine."

I couldn't hear any replies, but I was adamant I would do whatever I had to find a cure or, failing that, a reason for it so that I would know what step I needed to take next.

The elevator passed the ground level and I slammed the brake lever, slowing it in time for Meier's level. I exited into a darkened corridor and looked about. Not far away was an overturned chair. I grabbed it and stuck it in the elevator doorway to make sure it couldn't be called away.

Around to my right, pale electric light spilled from what I assume to be Meier's room. I didn't know how much time I had but I quickly strode inside and began looking around.

I was surprised to find every wall covered in maps of the galaxy, with assorted astronomical names and numbers. Lines had been drawn, calculations noted, areas circled, and complicated equations hastily scrawled in white chalk on the green walls. I could tell, from some of the more faded scratches, that this was where they must have worked out the planet's location.

It was then that I realized the newer calculations included time. I blinked at not having thought about that. The Einstein-Rosen bridge was not just a connection between space, it had to be across time as well.

I tried to remember what I knew about gravity and time; in case it was relevant. That foreign world was slightly heavier. Would it have an effect? The greater the mass, the slower the time in the gravity well and the faster the relative time outside it.

Was the portal leaking time? Is that why Solon had aged faster, and her wound had healed so quickly? As well as the disease spreading across Meier's body quickly. It might have been the bacteria, but time speed now seemed more likely to me. It wasn't just microwave radiation.

I turned to a bench that sat in the middle of the room with another galactic map. But this one was different. It not only showed the stars where they were now, but hand draw spots had been added with notations indicating the positions of the stars in the future. I recognized some of the equations came from works by Lindblad and Oort pertaining to galactic rotation. I knew our galaxy fully rotated once every 225 million years or so, yet I wasn't sure why this was relevant.

Then, as though intuition had caused me to look at one set of calculations again, I discovered the truth. The door definitely opens on a planet in our future. One which could be considered to be 25,000 years in our future. The excitement at this revelation that we time traveled as well, quickly gave way to a churning sensation again, as though I was missing something important.

What was it this time?

I peered closer at the added stars trying to work out what Meier had been trying to do. It was then that it hit me. His additional stars weren't the new positions of the nearby stars. They were stars that would be at that point in 25,000 years' time. Meier had included the future positions of the stars after they'd continued their rotation around the galaxy for 25,000 years, superimposed over the current positions. As I began looking for Sol the hairs rose on the back of my neck. My intuition had already told me what my mind refused to consider.

But Meier had made it plainly clear. A red line had been dug into the paper, scarring the distance between Sol's current position to Sol's future position in 25,000 years' time. It might have been just an idle line drawn for amusement, but the calculations next to it were clear.

The world we had visited was Earth, in the far future. Whatever those creatures were, the fact that their shape was so familiar to human body parts was because they must be human in some way. Was it our future evolutionary form?

I found a chair and sat down, shaking, my thoughts in turmoil.

Unconsciously, we expect humanity to continue getting more and more attractive. If we look back to Cro-Magnon man or even Neanderthal, the improvements are noticeable. Less hair, healthier skin, longer lives. I was sure Meier had expected, deep in the core of his being, to see glowing angels in our future. It wasn't the visit that had sent him mad. It was the record of the star positions and his calculations. Confirming that we end up as floating, lichen-eating breasts must have sent him spiraling into madness.

I briefly considered the evolutionary steps needed for this to happen. Positive mutations in sexual attractiveness lead to new evolutionary traits. Brighter feathers, more colorful fur, healthier physiques. The only thing I could think of was the human male's obsession with bigger breasts will eventually lead to humanity becoming floating mammary glands in the sky. But it takes two to tango, as they say. Women's interest in more attractive men would also have played a part. What did the males of this future species evolve that women wanted now? How did it lead to men being just square breasts as well? Why did they float? To escape mountain bears? I honestly had no idea.

It didn't make sense to me that we'd end up just floating and licking lichen. Was this somehow caused by a mad scientist? Playing around with our DNA? Or some nuclear explosion causing a mutation? Was it a choice? Thinking back, I recognized the grassy mountain range. Of course, it was the future Tatra Mountains. No snow, a lot more grass, but recognizable now that I could see it. But, where did the plateau come from? Was there some kind of tectonic upheaval, or was it that the land had fallen away in subsidence? I could only hazard a guess.

Certainly, 25,000 years was way too short for normal evolutionary mutations. What could have caused the human race to evolve so quickly?

I was about to run my glove through my hair, forgetting I still had my suit on, when I saw that it now looked to be too tight for my hand.

* * *

The elevator stopped and I looked about, fearful that Solon would attempt to get her revenge. But, I was relieved to see that she sat patiently waiting beside the microscope. She'd removed her suit and most of her clothes and was staring forlornly at the large bulge that had already swallowed her leg and was rapidly expanding across her waist.

She looked up at me as I approached. "You're here because you've got it, too," she said, matter-of-factly.

"I'm here because I want to help, and to tell you what I found. And secondly, yes, because I also have it, whatever it is, and we need to be quarantined."

"If the door remains open, there's a risk of this infection spreading to the population."

"Yes. I've been to Meier's room. Studied his calculations. Worked out what he discovered. Probably even why he went mad." I took a deep breath and prepared to give her the disturbing news. I did hope she wouldn't go mad like Meier, though with the infection already ballooning both her legs, perhaps I was too late. "That's not a foreign planet, Henryka. That's Earth at another point in its galactic orbit. You connected the door to itself in a future time."

Solon blanched, coughed, then gave a shuddering sigh. "So, no answer to the alienus question then. But, surely, if they were even partly human, we could have communicated."

It was then that inspiration struck me, and I realized how the air cows had been communicating. "I believe they already have."

"I don't understand."

"What if you're at this point because you followed your intuition to be here. I found your office easily due to mine. But what if intuition or even inspiration is the way the air cows communicate? Sending a need across space and time so that you would have no choice but to follow the steps to open a door. Every inspired action you took led you to connecting with them so that they could then send you the inspiration to do it!"

"That suggests predetermined futures. I'm against those."

"Even so, let's say they have caused us to be fated to meet them via the door. What then?"

"They exist because we met them and brought the infection back to change the human race to cause their existence!"

"Right! So, as you're not into predetermined futures, we need to close that door, now! Tell me how it works."

Solon grunted, coughed, swore, then looked up at me. "Fine. Here's a summary. We scientists talk about opening a wormhole and sending someone through this 'tunnel' across the stars, and how humans would never survive the radiation during the 'journey'. But it doesn't need to be a tunnel. If you could find a weakness in the fabric of space that can connect to another weakness, it only needs to be photons thick." She carefully pointed at the door. "The thinner the door, the less exotic matter you need to keep it open."

"Does the exotic matter create the time spillage?"

Solon grunted. "I suspected that. No, I had a theory that the galaxy contains a massive gravity well at its center that it rotates around. It's possible that crossing from here to another area is somehow influenced by it. We may be being affected by something so big light doesn't escape. Then again, I hadn't calculated the world was already in the future. Perhaps it is being kept open by the kinetic energy of two timefields rubbing against each other."

"You know, if you could somehow prove gravity wells exist, Einstein would be shocked. He'd be more likely to believe your wormhole."

Solon grinned at this.

"So, whether it is gravity or time or both keeping it open, how would you disrupt the exotic matter?"

"You just need normal matter. It interferes with the equilibrium. In a tunnel, a little would break it. You'd never get past the throat. But a stable door, photons thin? I've no idea."

"Gottfried said you'd need a human sacrifice. What if he meant you needed a human to sacrifice himself in the door to shut it down?"

It was then that I saw Solon had got the gun. She pointed it at me. "And now, with Gottfried's body turning into an air cow, there can be only one possibility."

I held up my hands. "What? No! Any non-exotic matter, right? We could shove tables, chairs in there. Anything."

"I'm afraid not."

I stared incredulously at her. Had the infection begun affecting her brain already? "Why?"

"I worked it out. To shut it down you need matter from both sides. The only thing that contains matter that exists both there and here is us."

I stepped back from her. "But what does that mean? One of us stands in the middle of the doorway and remains stuck until it dissolves? We'd be cut in half!"

"Well," Solon grinned with a slightly evil look in her eye. "You would be."

I strode quickly across to her and wrestled the gun from her fingers on her right hand before she had a chance to react. It felt lighter. She'd already removed the magazine.

"Really, Thomasz? You really thought I'd shoot you?"

"Well." Before I had time to react, now that I was close enough for her to do it, she cut my suit arm with a knife, held by her left hand. I felt the cold steel strike bone and turned, shocked at her behavior. It was then that my muscles began to freeze. The numbness spread quickly.

"You're much more use to me alive," she said, struggling to stand over me.

"Are you crazy?" I said, my speech beginning to slur on my right side. "It feels like…curare. The muscle relaxant. It stops everything! The lungs, the heart. You've killed me!"

I lost control of my body and crashed to the floor. Solon towered over me.

"Come now, Thomasz. I'm a scientist. I gave you an exact dose. Enough to make you almost immobile, but not enough to stop your heart."

I tried to remember my reading of curare. A toxin from South America. Depending on the medically administered dosage it can last from thirty minutes to eight hours. Some splashed on a knife that might have been wiped by clothing should mean just thirty minutes.

But thirty minutes would be enough for whatever she had in mind.

Darkness took me, and when the poison had done its work, and I was awake again, I found myself tied to the hell door. Incredibly, Solon's body had become round and bulbous, and her head had grown distinctly browner.

"It looks like the transformation is almost complete," I said, ignoring my predicament for the moment.

"I'm sorry, Tomasz. As much as this pains me, figuratively, literally and emotively, I have to do this." She lifted up her cane and pushed hard against my stomach. Immediately, I felt a cool breeze from the future Earth on my buttocks, and the burn of the door on my stomach.

"If I hold you there long enough, your normal matter will disrupt the exotic matter and the door will close permanently."

I only had one chance. If I could make her see, in time. I could feel pieces of myself dissolving like melting icebergs. "Evolution. The connection is over 25,000 years in the future. Not enough time for humanity to evolve into something like the air cows!"

Solon ignored me and pushed harder.

"Right now. The air cows exist in the future because they were created here by them sending their disease back to our time. A paradox. A time loop. We need to break it otherwise, this, now, will condemn humanity to that fate then."

The cane was lifted off me and I pulled myself back into

the room. I could feel my suit burning from the microwave radiation, but I had no other choice. If I stayed in the door I would die.

"What is the solution?"

"We blow up the door, and us with it. It's the only way to save humanity. You have the grenade."

She shuffled back and forth, a tear coming unbidden to her swelling face. "The Nobel was so important to me for so long."

"Yes."

"But now it doesn't matter. None of this matters. I'm turning into an air cow and my experiment could end the human race. Not particularly award worthy."

"No."

The she snarled. "But I have to shut down this goddamn door first! I could open another one somewhere else. Start again!" She lunged at me and with all her strength pushed me bodily into the door. I fell through to the other side, my covered head gasping methane laden air while my body remained on the other side, arms, legs and stomach providing normal matter to the door.

It was then I noticed what she had strung up my arms with. Rope. Possibly from tarred hemp. Organic. Could I use that? I pulled my left leg hard where the rope had been circled around my ankle. Twisting it to the side I was able to pull my foot through enough that the only thing passing through the door was the rope. I adjusted other parts of my body accordingly, and found myself, bizarrely, hanging in midair in front of the doorway on that future Earth. A new cloud of air cows paid me no heed.

Suddenly my right hand came free, and my body twisted

sideways, uncomfortably, the momentum throwing my left back into the door. I found my flexibility had become limited. Something was slowing down my ability to move. The cane also moved further forward, and I grabbed it quickly, pulling it through and dropping it to the ground. I noticed the red of the door had changed to a more pinkish color, and I began to hope that this meant it was getting weaker.

I then noticed my glove and sleeve had split; the swelling having taken over my arms. I wondered why there was no pain from the transformation. Was it at the DNA level? Something that was transformative rather than invasive?

Finally, I began to understand what was happening. We were turning into air cows, but to prevent us from dying during the transformation, we had to hibernate. No movement would be allowed while it took place. Bones would be dissolved, organs replaced, toenails and hair subsumed. The only way for that to happen safely is if the body created a cocoon. That's what was happening. And, strangely, I could feel myself being digested. The weight around my middle had reduced and tightened.

But then, what did this mean? Could there be future humans with cities, spaceships, advanced technology and then, at the end of their life, they transform into these bulls and cows, like bacteria-based butterflies, essentially having another life? We couldn't possibly understand the extra-terrestrial reasoning for our thinking in thousands of years' time. There was no way of assigning our belief systems or our laws to the situation. Perhaps this had been decided over centuries by the older population. A solution to gaining a long life. Old age, rather than retirement, or dying in a hospital somewhere, could mean a new experience in the sky. Perhaps these transformations had been designed by future humans and without the intervening years and inoculations for the younger populations, we'd caught it rather than having it turned on.

It might have been the cocoon or perhaps I'd come to accept my demise. There were so many happy people in the world that just fished all day and did nothing else. Here was my opportunity to do nothing else but float and eat lichen, and perhaps the occasional dalliance with one of the balloon girls. Hanging there, I began dreaming of this future, then realized the air cows had turned towards me.

This was their communication. They weren't using language. They were using feelings. And now I was feeling peace and contentment.

I struggled to snap out of it.

Then the other ropes snapped, and I fell completely through to that future Earth.

Moments later, to my utmost surprise, Solon joined me, wearing a lab coat with bulging pockets. I stared at her. Was she going to try lifting me up and throwing me through? Had she come to finish the job? I no longer cared.

The cocoon had stopped at her waist, and she grinned again, as though her attack on me had never happened. "Of course," she mumbled. "There's plenty of matter on this side." She saw my contented face. "You worked it out? A cocoon?"

I nodded.

"You've accepted it?"

I nodded again.

She sighed. "I haven't." She pulled out a vacuum flask

and poured some of it on my arms before putting the lid back on quickly.

I leapt up realizing it was liquid nitrogen. "Are you insane?"

"Liquid nitrogen disrupts the intramolecular disulfide bonds of a cocoon. It'll buy us some time.'

Now awake and alert I was secretly grateful. I wasn't ready to become an air cow, yet.

Solon began pulling rocks and dirt from the surrounding area and creating a wall. Animosity forgotten, I quickly helped her. When the stone wall was built, we pushed it so that the edges of the rocks were just inside the portal, leaving a small space at the top. I did enquire why a space was needed, but she simply said, 'one moment'. The rocks glowed and sparked from the radiation and the door became almost white. Solon then pulled out the M43 grenade, pulled the wire, and tossed it through the opening. We quickly stood to the side.

The door shifted from pink to orange, yellow, green, blue, purple and then, with what looked like a lightning strike, exploded, showering the burnt area in front of it with cut pieces from the stones. Moments later the hole faded to reveal the burnt side of the hill behind it.

"What would have happened if we had entered the door from the other side?"

"Ended up in the concrete of the building, most likely." She kicked the ground with her swollen foot and sighed. "That's it then."

"How long do you think we have?"

"Before we can't move anymore? No idea. This flask contains just one more application."

"If we're quick, we could go up the mountain and look around, see if there's a city nearby that can halt the cocooning process. Maybe join the future society, make a life here."

Solon nodded. "I never thought there could be something like that, so I never looked. That's why I needed your big picture thinking. Maybe we will find something. But, if we don't, becoming air cows isn't such a huge disaster. If we can retain our consciousness, make observations, satisfy our scientific curiosity…"

"Agreed," I said.

Together, shuffling and supporting each other, discussing a wide range of subjects to keep our minds off our impending evolution, we headed up the mountain.

El Peligroso

Robert Walton

I sometimes wonder why I climb on El Capitan. Its desperate routes obligate utilization of micro-molecular holds not visible to folks over thirty - like me. There are also those toad green moments of envy when some otter-sleek newcomer flashes the latest most difficult problem.

Yet I still dream of possibilities. New Route, you sloe-eyed temptress, I hear your call. Even though I detoured around climbing greatness and achieved a level of skill that might be described as advanced mediocre, I have found a new route on the Captain.

Airy wastes gape below me. The crux awaits my next step. My right foot is comfortably camped on a centimeter-wide edge. Secure, I indulge in that sweetest climber's vice - procrastination - and take in the view - pale, sun-splashed granite and blue sky.

A bulge rears above me. I can just snake my left arm around its sensuous curve and hook one finger over a rounded knob. A pull-up followed by a leaping thrust of my right hand into a blushing, adolescent crack will put me past the problem. The sequence is logical and elegant, flowing through my mind as smoothly as swift water over river stones.

The move's difficulty, however, is at least three grades higher than the best I climbed when I was twenty-two, many years and unnumbered beers ago. My internal reality check tells me I'm not going to make it. Time to retreat - I can always go on a diet and come back in a few months. Sure.

"Yo!" a voice sounds from slightly above and to my right. I turn. A beautiful young woman is hanging off of tiny crystals as if she were standing on a sunlit sidewalk. An icicle of recognition melts over my heart. The young woman is Delilah Lee Sanchez, rock climbing's brightest star. A dozen of her routes have never been repeated. She's apparently putting one up now. Right next to mine.

"Hello." I croak. "New route?"

I watch old movies. I give her my "Aw shucks" Robert Redford grin. "It's nothing too amazing."

"Looks hard." Her forearm muscles possess a leopard's silky lethal strength. She should be stressing on these small holds, but not the slightest quiver ripples her chocolate colored skin.

I shake my head. "Nah."

Her eyes sparkle. I'm a liar and she knows it. "Maybe we can have a beer later?"

Her smile gets wider. "I was hoping we could!"

Really? Why does the best climber in the universe want to have a beer with me? That's a question that deserves further thought, but not now. My foot is trying to leave its edge. Time to go. I give her Redford again. "Later, then."

She nods. "Later."

There's nothing left to do. I launch into the crux with her watching. The first two moves seize my consciousness with implacable granite claws and I forget about her. My muscles exert subtle, harmonized pressures through fingers and toes. I flow upward and am filled with that pre-lightning bolt imminence of a move beyond the edge of my ability.

I should say something about my shoes. I wear old, specific bond Sportivas, not the new variable bond Astaris.

I'm not a purist, but the Astaris turn climbing into little more than vertical ice-skating. Once properly adhered to rock, they cannot come loose until the molecular bond is reduced. Attachments with a strength of up to 200 kilograms per square centimeter are possible. This seems hardly fair. A climber can't fall.

Also, I had a bad experience with them when I first tried them out. I lost my hands while climbing a large roof and ended up hanging by my toes. I couldn't regain my holds and had to wait for my partner to quit laughing long enough to use the electronic remote on my shoes so I could fall before my earlobes popped.

The final thrust is upon me. I begin, though a small blackbird of doubt flutters at the edge of my awareness. My fingers, by the way, have not been surgically altered. I know it's an easy procedure and many climbers have had it done. Super-adhesive pads on one's fingers and patches of skin otherwise tougher and more abrasive than that of a mako shark can only help on the highest difficulty climbs. Still, there are trade-offs. A friend of mine had his right hand modified in this manner and the level of his climbing immediately rose two grades. However, he was also in love. In a moment of passion with his beloved, he forgot his alterations with unspeakable results.

Like an anemone's tentacles swaying gently in a deep blue current, the fingers of my right hand caress the crack. My body stretches tighter than violin strings, my muscles more rigid than the rock before me. My mind overflows with the perfect harmony of complete concentration as white adrenalin light explodes in my mind. It is there. The key hold is there. Half a centimeter more and it is mine. I lunge - too far.

The blackbird becomes an ebon vulture. It swoops into my mind as my ultimate effort crumbles. My fingers slide off the hold and out of the crack. My feet fly free of the rock and I arch over a thousand meters of emptiness.

My fall is in slow motion at first. Delilah's face registers surprise as I float past her.

Two other climbers are climbing roped fifty meters below and to my right look up as I fall past them.

The leader grins. His partner's raucous, taunting cry, "Crater-crater-crater!" chases me.

Climbers falling from El Capitan can expect no sympathy. High above, I see a bright speck detach itself from the wall. It is Delilah. She is diving after me. What can this mean? She scarcely knows me!

Wind whistles for my attention. I look down. My velocity is terminal, and the ground is near. It is covered with the usual litter of rock shards and boulders. I prepare myself by straightening my body and extending my hands, by taking that diving posture that always looks somehow prayerful. My fingertips stretch for the ground as it rockets up to meet them. The end is quick, so quick that I fail to see it. I am suddenly plunging through darkness.

This is my first fall from El Capitan and, though I've been informed of the details, I'm a little unsure of what will happen next. The Captain, of course, is in the large orbital complex know as Mountain High. Who in the Twenty-first Century would have dreamed that such an artifact would be constructed, mountain resort in space? Two hundred years later, close to forty- five million people live and work in the

L-5 residence colonies. They live in vacuum, but they crave earthly recreations.

Mountain High's heart is an intricately balanced group of chondritic asteroids. The largest structural members ever manufactured by humankind were used to bind them together. Around them is a honeycomb shell, containing atmosphere. On them lie facilities for every sort of mountain sport: skiing, snowboarding, bobsledding, hang-gliding, jet-assisted ski jumping and climbing.

The climbing is unequaled in quality even in Yosemite or Afghanistan. Seven silicate walls - mixtures of granite, feldspar, quartz and pegmatite - rise from a common base. They differ in angle and therefore in difficulty. The hardest is El Capitan, named for its forbear in Yosemite. The original's uppermost two hundred meters can still be seen above the crystalline waters of Lake Trump. Submarine tours of the drowned valley are very popular. Mountain High's Captain offers hard climbs that range upward into as yet unrated explorations.

My fall is becoming tedious. The plunge through the holographic "floor" of the valley was exciting, but this flight through dim light as my velocity decreases is not inspiring. Ah, there's a yellowish glow below me. I'm nearing Mountain High's lower pole in the low-grav section. A flashing target, alerted by my proximity, blinks its welcome. I turn in air and extend my feet. Air whispers like a blown kiss and I sink knee-deep into the shock-absorbing landing pad. My two-kilometer fall ends without even a whimper, much less a bang.

I straighten as the foam recovers its shape. A cry of "HOOOOOO-Wheeeeeeeee!" sounds above me. My God,

I've forgotten about Delilah. I glance up and see that she'll miss landing on me by ten meters. I smile and wave.

Her body slants down into the absorbent foam, sinks deep and then bounces from the foam's embrace. She slide-steps toward me grinning, her eyes full of star-sparkle. "I've got to do that again!"

"You've never fallen off El Capitan before?"

A wrinkle almost appears on her brow and she shakes her head. "No. I've fallen a couple of times during roped climbs, but never on a free solo, never all the way like that."

The long list of her first ascents on the Captain, many of them rope-less, passes through my mind. I shake my head in wonder - no falls. I suddenly realize that I'm not holding up my end of the conversation and stammer, "Want a beer?"

She brushes my wrist with strong, slender fingers. "I'd love one!"

* * *

The Crystal Crag, though in space, is the ultimate mountain bar. The best from every sport meet, drink, laugh and preen. Delilah and I pass from the brightness of the slideway into the Crystal's cavernous, pine-scented main room. We step past a holo-fire flickering in the stone fireplace. Above an oak mantel longer than a diving board, hang crossed ice axes, their oiled ash handles sending golden gleams of reflected firelight into the room. I repress an urge to touch them. Wood is rare in space and the satin-smooth antiques pull all climbers' fingers to them.

One belonged to Edmund Hillary.

We plunge deeper into the crowded room, heading for the tables in the rear. I see Charles, a friend of mine, sitting with members of his synchronized base-jumping team.

Charles and I climbed a lot together until he became involved in this specialized sport. The peril of falling while attached to four other people left me cold. Not to mention the fact that the stylized moves, obligatory strobe lights and costumes create the potential for true embarrassment, aside from the threat of terminal disaster. Night jumps, with their spectacular pendulum moves, are amazing. Charles and his partners are Olympic hopefuls. I wave to him. He nods back.

I turn to Delilah. The holo-fire's light shines in her eyes, reflects warmly from the full curves of her face. I am charmed, more than charmed. Entranced would be a good word.

She indicates an open table. "Shall we sit here?" "Ah, Sure." I close my mouth. "Beer?"

"Heineken's"

I punch her order into the table's monitor and order a Moon-duster for myself. Almost immediately the table hums and two snowy-frothed mugs rise on its central platform. Delilah grasps her glass and lifts it to take a sip. I smile and reach for mine.

A solid punch jars my right shoulder. Beer slops over my hand. "How's it going, Byron?"

What would life be without enemies? They are the jalapeno peppers in the mild cheese enchilada of existence, no? They intrude with their capsaicin rasp just when life promises to become sweet and prove irrefutably that the universe is indeed imperfect.

"Byron, babe, I saw you fall. Ugly, man!"

I turn and look up into the venomous blue eyes of Hans Hoffman. Ego pollutes every human activity, especially sports, and most especially those sports in which competition can turn deadly. Hans resents me because my reputation, though modest, is better than his. I say nothing.

Hans piles on. "Bet you thought you were on a new line? Hah! I did it already."

He lies. He's waiting for me to object so he can hit me. I am a man of modest dimensions. Hans is somewhat larger and more muscular than a mountain gorilla. I don't like being insulted, but I know my own limitations.

His face looms over my shoulder like a pale thundercloud. "Can't you hear anymore, Byron?"

I shrug.

"It's not polite to just sit there without answering, dude. I don't like it when people are rude to me, especially you."

Yes, especially me. Feeling like a silvery delicate insect caught in an ancient and malign web, I rise to sacrifice blood and teeth upon the altar of masculinity. Delilah's hand on my arm stops me. She stands and faces Hans.

"Delilah! I didn't see you!"

Delilah's eyes grip him like stony hands. "He's with me, Hans. Why don't you leave?"

Hans straightens, swallows and nods. "Sure, Delilah, sure. See you around." He turns and disappears into the bar's remotest shadows.

I sigh with relief and amazement. "Thanks! You saved me from disproving my manhood."

Delilah grins in answer and sits back down.

"How come," I pause and search for the right words, "he departed so meekly?"

Delilah's smile, almost shy in its delicacy, again illuminates her face. "Tae-Kwon-do is part of my training. I'm good at it. Hans knows that."

"Oh?"

"After a climb we did together last year, he put his hands where he shouldn't." "Oh."

"He won't do it again." I take a sip of beer.

"You feel like climbing tomorrow?" "Yeah, what time?"

"Is seven too early? Let's catch a shuttle to the moon."

* * *

I've always liked the moon, but it gives the shudders to many a hard woman and man.

Remote, high quality, high standard rock climbing in an airless environment, well away from the moon bases and any chance of speedy rescue requires the highest competence and commitment. Sharp edges? We're talking swords and razors. Climbers have lost their air often enough on lunar big walls. It's not the best way to go.

Delilah's suit lights swiftly recede above me. Her lead will end in 200 more meters when our monomolecular stressed ceramic line runs out. Don't ask me why it's so flexible, but, believe me, it curls like a baby's hair. More important, it retains its strength (7,000 kilograms, static) and its flexibility right down to a few degrees above absolute zero. Nothing less than an industrial grade laser will cut it. My suit instrumentation tells me that the current temperature is about minus 140 degrees centigrade. It will rise drastically when we hit the sunlight toward the top of our wall.

A chirp in my ear calls my attention to my Black Diamond out-world belay and rappel device - the Cobra. Delilah's rate of advance has exceeded the maximum rate I set earlier. I adjust it and then check the automatic coiler. It's functioning flawlessly, but I've seen too many incredible tangles to trust it for very long on its own. I look back at the

Cobra. Its lights are all green, small cat's-eyes of reassurance. Though more complex than the coiler, I trust it a great deal more. I've seen it hold 200 meter falls, absorbing enormous shocks, slowing the rope dynamically. The temperatures involved in airless climbing necessitate the use of the static, monomolecular rope. Shock absorption and control are entirely a function of the Cobra. The rope does pass through the space-gloved fingers of my right hand, but that's mostly symbolic.

I look up. Delilah has disappeared around a corner. A small butterfly of doubt flutters in my stomach. It's been awhile since she put any protection in. Low-gravity falls are deceptive.

They're slow at first, but lethal velocities build up quickly. Suit design limits can be exceeded by the shock of a rather short fall. These moon rocks are shark's teeth, every one of them.

Her voice sounds in my ear. "I'm safe. Come on up." "Belay's off."

I disengage the Cobra and switch the coiler to retrieve. I remove the anchor - three spring-loaded camming devices - rom the crack in front of me. Two devices would make an adequate anchor, but redundancy is a climber's watchword.

"Climbing." "Climb."

I breathe cool, pine-scented air (I've got my suit's air unit set for High Sierras in the autumn) and insert my hands in a wide crack. What goes free, and moderately so, on the moon would exceed the outer edges of possibility on Earth. This crack proves hard even for the moon and it's not the crux. X-tee climbers' gloves are tough, sticky, and - within certain limits - flexible. I'm used to their limitations and manage to gain height by using a series of fist and hand jams. I reach more moderate rock and look down.

Starlight and Earthlight bathe the plain below in a cold, voluptuous glow. The blue-silver is cut around its edges by knives of black shadow. I smile. Here I am again, stealing a peek at what humans were never meant to see. A tug on the line reminds me that Delilah likes to keep moving.

I join her without further difficulty or sightseeing. She's actually found a stance in a triangular alcove. This climb, named Dawn Child, has precious few of them. I move up to her and clip in.

Her teeth flash behind her faceplate. "Nice going. We're almost up."

"Nothing to it."

"Hey," she pauses, "Mind if I take this lead?" "The crux?"

"Yeah."

"Sure." I don't even feel embarrassed. I knew when I agreed to go out with Delilah that we wouldn't be doing a tourist route. We aren't. Dawn Child is one of the three hardest routes yet done on the moon. Delilah is one of six climbers who can successfully lead this next pitch. I'm not one of the other five.

"Thanks. Are you ready?"

I switch on my Cobra. "Belay's good." "Climbing."

"Climb."

And she does. A strange mixture of anxiety and admiration ties my insides in knots.

She's using low-grav counter-pressure techniques in a shallow groove. Her feet are smeared on crystals too tiny to mention. She has no protection in and won't for some time to come.

Magically, gracefully, she moves up the overhanging wall, seeming to climb without effort, though I hear her fierce and desperate breathing over the open mike. Ten meters, fifteen, she reaches a knob she actually grip. She pauses and gasps for breath.

My throat tightens. This is it, the notorious leap. She must propel herself up and out for two meters in order to reach the lip of an overhang and the sharp crack that splits it. The low- grav technique is called a pull-up thrust mantel. Her only point of leverage is the flat knob her right hand now grips. .

"Byron?" Her ragged breathing has steadied a bit. "Going for it. Watch me!"

"Go."

Her right arm straightens in one smooth motion and her suited body surges up the blank section. Her left hand stabs for the crack, plunging plunge deep. Her right hand slots in above her left. She cries out.

Horror shows many faces to climbers and it grins at me now through a blue-green mist made luminous by Earthlight.

The mist is Delilah's air. "Delilah!" I scream.

"I popped it, Byron."

"The suit automatics?" I plead. All spacesuits have self-sealing capabilities, though these capabilities are limited.

"Slowing it down some."

Slowing it down lots or she'd be dead by now. "Can you get an anchor in?" "No."

"Delilah," I try to speak calmly as I disengage my Cobra

and tie her off to the anchor, "I'm coming up. I've got the external patch."

Her voice has an edge I've never heard before, "What to you plan to climb on?" "You."

Silence echoes from above.

"Hold on tight and don't pass out." Or freeze. Or let your blood boil up into the black fangs of that vacuum vampire.

I change my Cobra to its ascender setting and clip onto the rope. Only a few hot wires of doubt spark on the edges of my consciousness. After all, it is the moon. I weigh only twenty kilograms, gear included. And she's a strong woman.

I concentrate on smoothness, on floating up the taut rope like a cloud. Delilah says nothing. I know she's concentrating too, trying to turn herself into a piton, trying not to think about her thinning air. How far up Everest is she now?

I reach her. A diamond-hard razor blade of moon-rock took her high on her left forearm as she made the dynamic jam. It cut through the suit just above the tough glove material. An X- tee climbing suit has a number of safety features and backup systems. Delilah has about gone through all of them. The self-seal goo has partially closed the slice in the suit material, but it bubbles like baby spit as I watch. The secondary seal at her elbow is probably damaged as well.

"Now that you're here," Delilah gasps, "what are you going to do?"

"I'm going to climb over you, put an anchor in the crack, tie us on and use the patch." "Hurry, I'm seeing black spots."

I adjust my Cobra, put my hands on her hunched

shoulders and splay my feet wide to either side. "Brace yourself. I'm going to mantel up on you."

"Hurry," comes her thin whisper, "I'm cold."

I pull down slowly on Delilah's shoulders and raise myself to her waist, her neck. I shift my hands and move above her head. One of the beauties of low-grav climbing is the slowness with which one can accomplish power moves. The beauty is not apparent to me now, though some analytical corner of my mind is cognizant of the uniqueness of the situation. I'll laugh later if we both survive. I place my right foot on an edge above the overhang. It's not much, but on the moon it's enough. I pull up and stand.

My quick-draw anchor is in my left hand already. I thrust it into the crack's welcoming darkness and release the trigger. Anchored.

None too soon - Delilah is off. She swings in a slow arc below me and her weight comes onto the rope, onto me. My right foot slides off its edge. My right hand tightens in the crack and holds. So does the anchor, moon-cam #3.

I get feet onto edges again. I activate the coiler. It whines through the fibers of my suit like an old-fashioned dentist's drill, but starts hauling Delilah up. I ready the patch.

Her limp form, head is bent forward, comes within reach. Her helmet's faceplate is smeared with red. Trying not to think of what that could mean, I grasp her left arm and straighten it. I smooth the patch onto the jagged tear, make it conform to the contours of her arm and activate the seal. The atmosphere readout on her external suit controls flashes red. She's down to a few stratospheric gasps of air.

I plug my transfer tube into the emergency valve on her chest and push the transfer button. I've got enough air for both of us. We'll be a bit above 3,000 meters, but that's all right, I hope. That smear of red makes me cold down to the middle of my gut, but I can't do anything else.

I turn to the anchor. It looks lonely. I put in two more pieces, clip in and transfer the rope's tension from my device to the anchors.

"Hey, what happened?"

My heart freezes and then thuds wildly. "Delilah, you scared the shit out of me." "Sorry," she mumbles.

"What hurts?"

"My head. My arm."

"What about the blood?"

"Just a nosebleed. Looks like you got here in time. Thanks." "How's your arm?"

"There'll be a puncture wound and some freezing. I don't think it's too deep." "Can you climb?"

I can see her smile through the red-hazed faceplate. "Yeah, with one hand tied behind

me."

* * *

The shuttle eases into Mountain High's number fourteen bay. I glance at Delilah. Her left arm is wrapped in a blue heal-sack. She has been friendly since the finish of the moon climb two days ago, but she hasn't said much. Something is on her mind. She looks up.

"Byron?"

"Yeah?"

"I'm embarrassed about that mess I got us into."

I shrug. "Accidents happen. We got through it and it was a good climb." She touches my arm. "Will you climb with me again?"

The shuttle docks at that moment and the usual explosion of activity interrupts my answer. In several moments we're walking down a tunnel into pine-scented air. We step into brightness. Great walls rise above and around us.

Delilah tugs my arm gently and looks into my eyes. "You never answered my question." I sigh. "I think we were great together. I've rarely climbed so well. But..."

"What?"

I look away from her. "I'm beginning to like you a lot, maybe more than is good for either of us."

She squeezes my arm. I look into brown eyes as warm as a California morning. "Will you climb with me again?"

"Always."

We walk for several moments in silence. As we pass Vail Tunnel, the main passage to the ski areas, she looks up. "Hey, are you tired?"

"No, not really."

"Good. Let's go to bed." Oh, my.

* * *

I awoke and found Delilah's eyes on me. "Enjoying the view?" She grins. "I'll like it better after the view shaves."

I plump my pillow and start to roll over. "The view will make things better in an hour or

so."

She rises on her left elbow. "Have you ever considered doing a big X-Tee climb?" I turn back to her and shrug. "Not seriously."

"Would you like to do El Peligroso?" My eyes open wide. "On Miranda?"

She nods. "It's the biggest alpine wall in the solar

system, twenty-six kilometers of vertical rock, ice and who knows what else?"

"You mean it?"

She looks steadily at me.

I shrug. "You mean it. It's a long way to Uranus. I don't have that kind of money. Do

you?"

"I do. I've got a sponsor, a scientific expedition. The scientists want to explore Miranda's surface in person. They came to me because their itinerary includes a climb of El Peligroso. I checked out various partners and then…I came to you."

"I'm flattered."

"Don't be. You've done lots of different things and you don't freak out when things go wrong."

I smile. "Well, I haven't yet."

She grins. "You saved my ass on the moon. That counts." "Was that some sort of test?"

"No, I just wanted to see if we would climb well together." "And?"

"Great for me. How about you?"

I pull her close and we kiss. The kiss is among the best I've ever been a partner to, but, as with all kisses, it ends.

She shakes her head. "That's not what I asked. Do you want to climb hard with me?" I look down. "We climbed great together on the moon, but…"

"But what?"

"Peligroso is different. It might be more than I can handle. Nothing even remotely that long and hard has ever been done."

She raises my face with both hands and looks into my

eyes. "If it can be done, you and I can do it. Will you come with me?"

I take a deep breath. "Sure. I just wanted to be honest with you. I have doubts." She kisses my cheek and murmurs, "So do I."

* * *

Longsleep is what they call they call the induced hibernation used on lengthy outer solar system journeys. It's a lying euphemism. You wake up frozen with your head weighing forty pounds and every nerve ending screaming like a scalded cat. A cup of coffee rests on the table before me. I'd like to pick it up, sip from it, but if I stop holding my head up with both hands it'll crash through the table and break my knees. Like a hangover? A hangover isn't even in the ballpark.

Delilah divines my need, lifts the cup and holds it to my lips. I sip and swallow. There's hope. I sip again.

"Honey, you don't look so good."

A second sip of coffee arrives in my mouth. I might live.

"Byron? I've got some bad news."

I want to shake my head, but I know better. I utter a non-committal grunt.

Delilah takes that for polite inquiry. "I've met our boss. He's going to be tough work

with."

I grunt again.

"He's dictatorial, arrogant sarcastic and condescending. That's just for starters."

I try to frame a question. Dr. Paul Jenrath, our expedition leader, walks in at this moment. He's tall, thin, pale and bald. Ungenerous lips compress into a straight line below his sharp nose. His pale blue gaze flickers briefly my way. "I'm glad to see that you're finally conscious. Miranda is now visible."

He steps to a monitor and turns it on. Curiosity helps the coffee revive me. I glance up.

At some early point in its long and chilly life, this moon of Uranus was smacked hard by something almost as big as it is. Miranda blew apart and its gravity pulled the pieces higgledy- piggledy back together. These unimaginable geologic contortions left massive scars. On one of them, the solar system's biggest rift-wall is our climb, El Peligroso.

An expedition attempted to climb the wall fifteen years ago. Six top climbers made rapid progress to the twelve-kilometer level. Then they disappeared. Miranda is apparently not all that well glued together. Somehow, Peligroso swallowed them all. Their ship's crew searched well beyond the duration of the climbers' oxygen supply and found no trace of them and few clues as to what killed them. Speed, judgment and luck might get us up where our predecessors failed. I hope so.

Jenrath smiles toothily, but his eyes remain frosty. "We'll get started tomorrow. I trust that you feel up to it?"

I look at him bleakly but say nothing. Delilah says, "Of course, Doctor. "We'll begin scouting for a route."

Jenrath sniffs. "That won't be necessary. I've decided that already. A certain section of cliff is of interest to me and your job is to climb straight to it." He turns and leaves the room.

I glance at Delilah. She's biting her lower lip. Hard.

* * *

Delilah's voice rasps over the mike. "Watch me!"

"Got you." I check my belay device for the fourteenth time.

"The ice has gone powdery. I'm going to run it out for another fifty meters. I think it gets better up above."

"Go for it." Her suit lights are two hundred meters above me, more. I look down and breathe deeply, slowly. A fourteen-kilometer precipice would take one's breath away under ordinary circumstances. Nothing is ordinary about Miranda.

Great swathes of green ice glow with an eerie, undersea luminescence. Iron gray rock bands sprout gendarmes like a prizefighter's broken knuckles. Ledges, both miniscule and large, gleam with films of ancient ice dust. The bottom of the rift is in shadow darker than hell's own cellar.

I usually take great joy in a climb's scenery, even when I'm scared. Not now. Menace squats on me like a giant, its enormous haunches crushing my spirit flat. There's a minefield above us and the mines are as big as L-5 colonies. They are imbedded blocks of dark ice, protruding like teeth from the cliff's face. The smallest is a kilometer across. The blocks are embedded, but embedded how, and how much? My climber's instinct screams at me to move.

Delilah's voice mutters in my ear, "The ice is better. There's a ledge not much further on. It will do for a belay."

"Right." I swallow. "Take your time."

Jenrath, hanging from an anchor to my right, reminds me of his unpleasant presence. "We're close!"

Close? Close to what? The blocks? Interstellar space? I voice neither my irritation nor my doubts. I'm just the hired help. He has much better conversations with himself than he ever could with me.

Delilah comes on again. "This is strange."

"What?"

"This ledge looks like somebody carved it."

Jenrath shouts into his mike, "Touch nothing! I must join you quickly!" Delilah answers him, "I'll set an anchor and you can come up in a minute."

Jenrath kicks his front points into the ice and moves to my side. "I must go up next! Nothing must be disturbed before I can take measurements!"

Delilah speaks again before I can say anything inappropriate. "The belay's good, Dr. Jenrath. I'll wind you up on the haul rope. Don't touch anything! Byron, come up on your cobra and clean. The anchor is bombproof."

The haul rope tightens. Jenrath clips himself to it, unclips from our anchor and begins to rise. He says not a word in parting. I sigh. He's freight, obnoxious freight. We're on the longest, hardest alpine climb ever attempted and he could give a damn. This probably irritates me most of all. I take another deep breath. This is no time to stop paying attention because I'm annoyed.

I set my cobra device for self-belay and make sure the tension is correct. I use my laser tool to remove the first of the two X-tee ice screws, which comprise our anchor. The depth setting is slightly off. I adjust it and tackle the second screw. Especially formulated to withstand minus 200 degree Centigrade temperatures, they penetrate half a meter into solid ice. I work carefully. We'll need these babies again. I pull it, attach it to my harness and check my cobra.

Ready.

The enjoyable work of climbing on steep ice calms me. Forty meters out, I encounter another ice screw, the only piece of protection Delilah managed to place on this pitch. I remove it and move up three meters. Hell's frozen brass bells! It feels like crusted sugar beneath the points of my tools. Shivers dart up my spine. Just what is holding this cliff up? Not much.

Wonder at Delilah's courage while leading this death pitch grows in my mind. I focus and place my tools precisely. Time disappears until I reach solid ice and pull onto the belay ledge.

Delilah secures me to the anchor with a long sling of monomolecular. "Welcome." "Great lead."

"Thanks. I hope I never have to do anything like it again."

I look around. As ledges go, this one is a palace: five meters wide and three deep. I look up. A vast block of green ice is poised 500 meters above us, stuck into a band of pale powder ice. I glance back at Delilah.

She nods. "This place sucks."

It dawns on me that something is missing. "Where's Jenrath?" Delilah tilts her head. "Inside."

"Inside?"

"There's an ice cave. Somebody was here before us."

I ponder this. "The Plaskett expedition got this high?" "They didn't."

I look more closely at the ledge. "Melted?" "Yeah. It's a bivy, but no human made it."

The truth seeps into my mind like snowmelt. You mean?" "Whoever they were got this far, but no farther."

"How do you know?"

We're clipped to their rappel anchor. Look." A crystal ring protrudes from the ice. "It's harder than diamond."

"Damn! Jenrath took us on a Yeti hunt and didn't bother to tell us!"

"Yeah. He probably had secret information from the rescue mission's records." Jenrath's voice cuts across my dark thoughts. "Come here!"

Delilah nods. I scramble across the ledge, crawl into a narrow opening in the ice and into a large chamber. Jenrath is at its far end. His headlamp beam turns the walls deep turquoise and stabs down at the floor. I move closer.

Something glimmers from the ice in front of Jenrath. He mutters, "It's one of them, buried."

Something glitters to my right. I turn and a nova of white light blooms beneath my headlamp - a small implement fashioned from the same crystalline material as the ring outside. I pluck it up and attach it to my utility harness.

Jenrath mutters, "This should do it." I look up. He triggers a sonic vibrator before I can scream at him. A blast of focused sound powders the ice around the dead alien. I dive across the intervening space and knock it from his hands - too late.

Delilah screams, "Byron! The block is loose!"

Jenrath snarls at me and reaches for the vibrator. I grip his gloved hand. "You stupid shit! You just killed us!"

"Byron! Hurry!"

I release Jenrath and dive for the opening. Delilah points up. I look and see a silvery jet of powder ice spurting from the shadow beneath the giant block.

Delilah speaks softly, "The good news is that we aren't squarely under it. The bad news is that we're far enough under it to get flattened anyway."

The ice jet expands with the roiling slowness of a

squid's ink plume. Gravity here on Miranda is not strong, but, as is the way of gravity everywhere, it persists. The block begins its slide, accelerating in increments toward the base of Peligroso. We have between two and three minutes to ponder its monstrous plunge before it grinds us to paste.

"Got any ideas?"

I point. "That way?"

"Two hundred meters to get out of the fall line."

"More."

"I'll go." She takes an ice-screw off my suit. I shout. "Get out here fast, Jenrath!"

He scrabbles out of the cave. "What's the matter?"

"We've got to leave."

"We can't leave now! This is the greatest scientific discovery in human history!" "Not for long."

I point up. The block is sliding faster now, throwing out explosive darts of powder-ice.

Jenrath's face goes slack with horror.

Delilah grabs him and hooks him to our haul rope. "This ledge won't be here in two minutes. We're leaving."

I turn off my com and touch helmets with her so that we can speak privately. "What's the plan?"

"I'll traverse as far as I can." She pats the unused snow-blow deep anchors on her suit. "I'll plant this and then you two jump. Swing past me as far as you can and then plant your deep anchor. I'll pendulum to you."

"Will that be far enough?" She smiles. "We'll see."

I check my cobra. "Belay is good." "I'm climbing."

"Climb away."

Delilah plants the gleaming pick of her ax and begins. The ice is little more than frozen sugar, treacherous and begging to fail. Delilah's moves are those of a wispy spider, graceful and seemingly effortless.

But the effort is enormous. I can feel it along the rope, an electric current of exertion and terror pulsing in invisible waves. Her fear is a crab's cold claw plucking at her feet, pinching her muscles, but then I feel her spirit leap like a flame as she weaves a path through frost and nothing. This is the greatest climbing I've ever seen.

The chime on my cobra sounds as she passes a hundred meters. She pauses, raises the snow-blow and plunges it deep. Her voice sounds in my ears, "Off belay. The anchor is good."

"You're off. I'll hook Jenrath to me." "Hurry."

I clip myself to the scientist with a three meter-loop of monomolecular cord. I pluck his ax off his utility patch and place it in his right hand.

He opens his mouth. "What?"

"Don't talk! Listen! Dive out and down when I say three. Thrust as hard as you can. The ropes will come tight and swing us past Delilah. When our momentum slows, I'll plant my ax.

Then you plant yours too. Got it?" "Yes."

"If you screw up, we'll likely die." He nods.

I take a deep breath. "One, two, three!"

We dive. I glance up. The block is charging like a herd of rhinos, ice dust boiling up beneath stampeding feet. It's much closer than I'd hoped. The rope tugs as we reach the bottom of our pendulum and begin our upward swing.

Delilah sings out, "You're past me and you're clear."

I look up again. Delilah is not clear. The rhinos will stomp her flat in ten seconds, less.

I scream, "Delilah! Get out of there!" "Jumping now!"

We're no longer attached to Peligroso. This isn't good technique. I slap my ax back on my suit, grip the snow-blow and make sure its sling is clipped to one of my suit's attachment rings. I deactivate the anchor's safety, punch the laser activation tab and dial it to max penetration. I don't let my mind dwell on the fact that this will be so far beyond design limits that it doesn't even count as desperate. The snow-blow deep anchor's laser melts ice to a depth of two meters and plants a telescoping tube that freezes into place when the laser pulse fades. You're supposed to be standing still when you place it.

Delilah cries out. I look over my shoulder. Rhino dust has swallowed her. "Delilah!" "I'm okay. I can't see, but I'm okay!"

Jenrath yells, "I'm slowing down."

He is. So am I. Almost time to go to work. I've got to plant the snow-blow when I'm moving slowly enough for it to penetrate and hold. I have to do this before Delilah's weight comes on the rope. If I get it wrong either way, we'll charge behind the rhinos to the bottom of the wall.

I glance down. The block is moving faster, crushing ice and ejecting it in turquoise billows. There ought to be roaring and tortured shrieks, but there is only an eerie, underwater silence. Suddenly, Delilah shoots out of the spume, moving fast. The arc of her pendulum will put her directly below me in seconds. It's time.

I hold the snow-blow with both hands and reach high above me. I jab the prong into Peligroso and hit the trigger. Red light turns ice to blood. I rise even with the device and push hard. It plunges deep as the laser strobes off. Will it hold?

I reach the end of the anchor loop and the snow-blow stops me dead. Jenrath rises past me, reaches the end of his sling and gives the system an even harder tug. Delilah's weight and kinetic energy hit the snow-blow from the opposite direction. I close my eyes. A few seconds turn into years.

Jenrath's irritating whine sounds in my ears, "What now?"

I open my eyes. The snow-blow is holding. Jenrath and I are settling back below it. I whip out a regular ice screw and drive it in a few feet to the right of the blow. I clip to it and look down. The rhino ice block is now a diminishing blot on a vertical blue-green table. Delilah is already using her cobra to ascend the rope to us. I take a deep breath and close my eyes again.

"Honey, you okay?"

Delilah is next to me. She clips to our anchor. I look at her and feel strangely shy. It feels like years since we last spoke to each other. "I could use a beer."

"Me, too."

Jenrath intrudes. "What do we do now?"

She looks at me and shrugs. "Up or down?" "Down is too far."

She looks at the ice above and to our left. "That's much better." "Up?'

She nods. "Up."

* * *

The Pequod is a new ship, roomy and comfortable. I sit in its well-lit lounge with a beer at my elbow. Unfortunately, it will be my last one for three months, as we must enter long-sleep soon. I study the crystalline object I snatched from Peligroso's ledge, the only remaining evidence of humankind's first encounter with an alien civilization.

Delilah rests her fingers on my shoulder. "Is that what I think it is?" I nod. "An ice tool."

"So small."

"So strong." Its silvery smooth twenty-centimeter haft, cool against my skin, is apparently made of some alloy. Its molecules have been rearranged to make it incredibly tough. It might break if we hung the Pequod from its spike. It might not.

I turn it in my hand. It would afford a perfect grip for fingers much smaller than mine - or tentacles.

I hold the delicate tool up to the light. ""It has an energy source, too, and can reshape itself into different shaped tools." This will keep Jenrath's team busy for years."

Delilah rubs my shoulder, "I hope so."

"Me, too." I place the tool carefully on the table. "Hey, why so down?"

I shrug.

"We just made the biggest, hardest climb in history and pulled off the first ever double dynamic pendulum in the middle of it!"

I smile at her. "Both of which I hope never to repeat!"

She reaches down, strokes the tool with one finger. "I wonder what they're like?"

I cover her hand with mine and squeeze gently. I feel strangely sure that we'll find out.

After all, the makers of this tool are climbers. They'll be back to finish their route.

The Prison-house of Language

Elana Gomel

I did not speak until I was six.

My parents were offered the usual platitudes: *Einstein did not speak until he was in primary school* (not true); *did you try a body-based therapy* (the answer a horrified "no!"); *she will never shut up when she starts* (in high school, I would often go for days without opening my mouth; I still do). I was lucky, though, that my parents, being constantly on the move and totally wrapped up in each other, paid little attention to my disability. I was not diagnosed until much later in life. I was not medicated. When our three-person family settled down in some place for longer than a couple of months, I was given intermittent speech therapy, which produced no results whatsoever. I was not bullied in the various schools I attended; just ignored. When I reached adolescence, my exotic looks — green eyes and cocoa-colored skin — drew attention of boys, so I never lacked company. I liked sex because it precluded the need for conversation.

Language always felt, to me, like an invasion. When it finally came, it filled my mouth like a handful of grinding stones. I often experience a physical pain producing words: some words more than others. It has little to do with their meaning and a lot with their shape. Words like "love," "delegate," "serendipity," and "confabulate" make my gums bleed. Others, like "kismet" and "friendship," are puke-colored. Still others, like "starch" and "optimize," are glass-transparent, but can be dangerous if broken into sharp little syllables. Language, to me, is a dangerous and unwanted thing, a brutal intrusion into my inner space.

I became a linguist.

It'd be easy to say that I was looking for a language I could speak without spitting blood, but it would be an oversimplification. I can learn a new language in a week and retain it forever. Occasionally, I pull out a retired language from my mental storage and examine it, hoping that it has somehow matured into compatibility while fermenting in my mind. But this never happens. Swahili is the closest to a neutral means of communication I can use, but it still gives me a cluster headache. Standard Arabic is like chewing a rose-flavored gum: pleasant at first, but soon nauseating. English is the worst: rock fragments rolling in my mouth and battering my teeth. Even writing it requires wearing a mouthguard, so I won't shatter my expensive dental-work.

For a while, I tried to use a tablet to communicate. But the admiration of my classmates when I faultlessly answered any question asked by a randomized language program in the same tongue, aided only by my brash self-confidence, was too heady. Boys told me I had a beautiful voice. They say that Renoir painted despite excruciating arthritic pain. I convinced myself that I was like him — a solitary genius, overcoming the weakness of the flesh by the sheer force of will.

This, of course, had been before my father's death. Afterwards, I hugged my pain as a substitute. Or an atonement.

* * *

The call came as I was researching one of the recently extinct Australian languages, Bidyara. This was my own pet project that had nothing to do with my official job as a translator to the UN. I was trying to recreate the first language, the primal language spoken by our hominine ancestors. This is an idea universally considered to be antiquated, anti-scientific, and vaguely racist, on a par with the medieval attempts to figure out the language of God. Naturally, it became an obsession. I have been repeatedly told that OCD is part of my "condition." It is the only part I enjoy.

The window blinked into existence, overlaying the phonetic grid I was peering at, and the face of an old woman stared disapprovingly at my attenuated attire: knickers and a tube top. I knew she was old because her porcelain skin had that weird, glassy sheen that repeated gene-juve leaves in its wake. I actually like it and am looking forward to acquiring my own — in about thirty years *if* everything goes well with my stock portfolio. Rejuvenation does not come cheap.

"Dr. Abdoul?" the woman asked. "Dr. Sophia Abdoul?"

I was silent. I don't waste my limited speech tolerance on small talk. She knew who she had called.

The old woman sighed. She was generically beautiful, with one of those faces that, as Oscar Wilde had quipped, once seen, are never remembered.

"We would like to hire you," she said. "A special project, full non-disclosure, B1- pay-grade. Starting immediately."

I lifted a brow. Non-verbal communication is not painful, just irritating.

"The Peace Corps," she clarified.

The Army.

* * *

We are made by language. It has dug an impassable

trench between us and our animal brethren, who peer at us across this divide with their mute, opaque eyes. Animals have various communication systems, some quite sophisticated. But human language is structured quite differently from these systems. Note that I say "language," not "languages." All human tongues have the same underlying grammar. The old Chomsky theory that language is a sort of universal module, miraculously slotted into our brains at birth, has often been challenged, but never disproven.

Something went wrong when this slotting happened to my brain. My DNA has been mapped, and a number of mutations pinpointed. Some could be reversed. As with all gene-therapies, the consent for this reversal had to be given by the recipient at the appropriate legal age (which happened to be twelve in South Sudan, where my parents were stationed to monitor another interminable civil war that had come on the tail-end of yet another patented crop's failure). I was asked; at the time, I refused. My parents did not pressure me.

I still occasionally call my mother, blot out my end, and have exactly five seconds to look at her until, tired of fruitless "Who is it?", she disconnects and blacklists another disposable number.

* * *

The old woman's name was Major Stella Rostoff. The name, Russian in origin, did not suit her. On our way to the Project's location, I amused myself by figuring out what language she should be speaking as her mother tongue. I decided it should be Azeri, full of quick, bit-off words that sound like curses or commands.

She spoke English, of course, and badly, too: with

meandering sentences and unnecessary repetitions. Finally, I just asked for the relevant material to be downloaded to my implant and reviewed it in blessed silence.

As the result of this review, I had to risk a toothache by speaking.

"Why am I here?" I asked.

Stella looked at me in amazement.

"Your unique qualifications…" she begun.

"I am a linguist. This is brain science. Take me back."

I had reached my limit of pain-free speech and had no intention to continue unless I was paid, so I mutely ordered my AI to stop the car, which resulted in our fishtailing across the tawny-colored Mojave Desert. Fortunately, we had passed the electronic fence, plastered with threatening signs, some time ago, so there were no other cars to hit.

"Whoa, whoa!" Stella's AI returned us to the dusty tarmac and pulled off. "Didn't you get to the part about the after-effects?"

I had glanced at it, but now I called it up again. I reluctantly admitted that she may have a point. In any case, a second thought occurred to me: a B1-pay-grade was nothing to sneer at in the time of depressed markets. My portfolio was not doing as well as I needed it to be doing.

I stared at the faces of the volunteers. They all looked grey, somehow, and I wondered whether this was another side-effect or sheer exhaustion. A human being can go on without sleep for about seven days. After that, hallucinations, delusions, and severe cognitive impairment set in. Two weeks of sleeplessness kill rats and presumably humans. These people had been awake for at least four days, on the average. It was not because they could not sleep. It was because they refused to do so. They drank coffee until their heartbeats spiked up into the danger territory; they paced their rooms; they beat their heads on the wall; they stuck knives and scissors into their flesh to keep themselves from nodding off. But a person can only stay awake by the sheer force of will for so long. Eventually, they drifted off into slumber one by one. And when they did, they did not wake up.

I scrolled through the files to see how many of them were in a coma. It seemed more than sixty percent. The others were holding sleep off, but only just.

I risked another grind of words on my molars.

"How were they chosen?"

"Volunteers," Stella replied.

This was what the files said, but I did not believe it. I stared at her until she looked away.

"Refugees," she said. "Promised asylum."

This was interesting, if only because it confirmed what I had gathered from their names and faces: they were of all ethnicities and all mother tongues. And yet they all gabbled alike, producing an unending stream of the same gibberish.

It is actually quite hard to make up a language. Whatever mother tongue you originally spoke would emerge from under the artificial agglomeration of random sounds like the bedrock from under the swirls of windblown sand in the desert. And even if somebody came up with a truly new vocabulary, the essential structure of all human languages — the Chomsky module — would still be there. Examples abound: like a group of deaf kids in Nicaragua in the 1970s developing their own sign language, or the pompous tongues of bad fiction, from Elvish to Klingon.

But the sounds produced by the sleep refuseniks of the Project, while undoubtedly articulate and quite complex, did not fit any phonetic template I could think of. And they were uniform across the group, regardless of whether it was Rima from Lebanon or Augul from Xinjiang speaking.

"Translate?" I asked as the car sped across the baked landscape.

Stella gave me a contemptuous glance.

"The best AI translation programs," she said. "No results."

The subtext was that they would not bother with me if their precious machines could do the job. I could not argue with that.

The warm air, smelling of sagebrush and dust, caressed my face when we exited the car, having gone through the gauntlet of discreetly camouflaged security cameras. I like the dry calm of deserts. It is the wet heaviness of coastal cities that I have a problem with.

The Project was located in a sunken structure, whose mirrored dome was painted orange and dark rose by the garish sunset. I looked up into the pink sky as I followed Stella across the forecourt. There was nothing to see, of course. All that peering into the universe with powerful telescopes in search of a sign — and all in vain. The real thing had been hiding in plain sight within this glorified military bunker. Or rather, within the brains of the refugees that cowered in their brightly lit cells, afraid to go to sleep.

The aliens.

* * *

There is a story in Herodotus that Pharaoh Psamtik I, eager to know what the first language spoken by humans was, ordered two babies to be brought up by deaf-mutes. Supposedly, the children started spontaneously babbling in Phrygian. Subsequently, other curious tyrants repeated this atrocious experiment. The primordial tongue varied according to the expectations of the culture: Hebrew, Latin, even, in some versions, French. Now we scoff at those crude attempts to dig down to the roots of humanity. Children reared with no linguistic interaction would not speak at all. And yet…there must have been the ur-language, spoken by the original band of hominines who rolled over the planet, exterminating their mute cousins. Wouldn't you like to know what it sounded like?

But perhaps an even more interesting question is: what was there *before* language? The empty slot of the Chomsky module: had it truly been empty before the plug of the universal grammar was shoved in?

* * *

I showered off the dust of the desert journey in the tiny bathroom of my assigned quarters, which contained a bed, a wardrobe, and a sim-window. Irritatingly, it showed surf on the sodden beach. I tinkered with the controls and succeeded in calling up a forest scene with a spastic rabbit that twitched alarmingly, due to some programming glitch. Still, it was better than the alternative. The quarters were Spartan, to put it mildly, but thanks to my upbringing, I am very adaptable. My parents, observers for the UN Human Rights Committee, had been very relaxed about such things as tables, chairs, and indoor plumbing.

At least the dome was warm. I hate layers of clothing and go naked when the occasion calls, which has the added advantage of signaling to potential sex partners without having to go through the torture of small talk. But the only people of the Project I had met so far had been Major Stella and a glum neurobiologist called Aziz, who exhibited all the symptoms of an incipient nervous breakdown. Neither of them was to my taste, so I put on shorts and a top and went exploring.

I was stopped by a soldier before I got very far, and it took a call to Stella to straighten things out. She showed up in person, looking peeved.

"I thought you'd want to go over the recordings first," she said.

"Sleep," I started to say, but seeing incomprehension on her face, realized I was speaking in Old German. It fills my mouth with a meaty aftertaste, but it was better than the rattling stones of English. My teeth were already throbbing.

"Sleep," I repeated, determined not to say another word, but she understood. Perhaps I had underestimated her. Even stupid people are improved by experience, and who was to say how many years our blond, ponytailed major had spent in the military?

She nodded reluctantly.

"Yes," she said, "they cannot hold out much longer without sleep. And no matter what we do, we cannot wake up them up. Scans show alterations in the frontal lobe, but unlike any other pathology we have ever seen. Very well, try to talk to them. Follow me."

* * *

It all started with the Fermi paradox, of course. You know: if there are aliens, where are they? Tons of verbiage promising a solution; SETI programs; search for inhabitable planets…and nothing. Not a peep.

And then somebody had a bright idea. The name of that genius was blotted out in my records, but I did not care who it was. The consequences were all that mattered.

Perhaps, so the thinking went, aliens are in fact all around us, but we cannot see them because our perception is limited and skewed by language. It has long been argued that language conditions not only what we can say, but what we can think and see. The Sapir-Whorf hypothesis, it is called, though I prefer the poetic phrase "the prison-house of language." I don't remember its origin, but it has stuck with me and apparently with whoever was behind the Project. They suggested that we break down the prison-walls and let our perception roam free. Perhaps then, we can actually contact the aliens.

The idea sounded loopy to me, but the military was persuaded, though a more cynical interpretation may suggest that they just wanted to do something with the refugees accumulating in the island camps. So, the Project was set up. It had a code name, but everybody just called it the Project, which had a certain logic to it: if you want to get rid of language, use as few words as possible.

The details of the brain intervention that the subjects had undergone were too technical for me, but it was clear they involved switching off several genes involved in language acquisition, including the famous FOXP2, and switching on some dormant bits of DNA. Astonishingly, instead of just plunging the subjects into a coma straightaway, this brain-scrambling produced spectacular results. First, the so-called volunteers, who had apparently not known each other before the experiment, started falling asleep and waking up simultaneously, even when they were kept apart. Second, their dreams became synchronized, as well. Dream-recording equipment is still crude and unreliable, but they were able to obtain some spectacular footage, which I reviewed with increasing disquiet. And finally, though they lost the capacity to use their native languages, they did not stop speaking. Just the opposite: as the tapes showed, they gabbled incessantly. I was reminded of the glossolalia of charismatic sects, even though this oozing of agglutinated phonemes sounded more uniform than anything produced by ecstatic worshippers. But if this was a language, it was unlike anything else on Earth.

And this was where I came in.

* * *

Rima Habibi was a pretty, slim girl with brown hair and blue eyes like many Lebanese; the Crusaders' genetic legacy, more durable than the crumbling stones of Beaufort Castle. She looked underage to me, and I seriously doubted she was legally competent to give consent, but such niceties had been almost forgotten in the last decade of renewed political upheavals. She was wedged into the corner of her cell. Her hand was bleeding from where she had repeatedly struck it against the edge of the table. I crouched in front of her, despite the obvious disapproval of Stella, who hovered at the entrance with an armed guard peering over her shoulder.

I spoke to Rima in Lebanese Arabic, which, as opposed to other Arabic dialects, tastes of aniseed. It is my favorite, so I may have cheated by choosing her, though it quickly became clear that it made no difference, as she did not react at all. I was observing her carefully, and there was not even an unconscious twitch or eye movement, which always accompanies the sounds of a familiar language. I spoke to her in French. I even tried Armenian, even though her file stated she was a Christian Arab. No luck.

But she did speak, though it did not seem to be in response to what I said. She was gabbling on over me, pouring forth a flood of shocking syllables. I listened carefully for a while, and then I leaned forward and dabbed away the blood on her hand with an analgesic tissue I had brought with me.

I discovered myself on the floor, cartoon stars in my eyes, stickiness on my brow that split open as Rima's delicate hands smashed me into the wall. The armed guard was yelling as he pushed her face down on her cot while Stella tried to lift me up. I stopped the commotion by getting up myself and telling the guard to leave the subject alone.

When we were outside, I turned to Stella.

"It's not a human language," I said.

"You mean it's not one you know?"

"I mean it's not one anybody knows. It does not have the structure of a human language. It's outside the Chomsky module."

She frowned, looking dubious.

"It sounds articulate."

"So do thrushes' songs."

"And you can't translate it?"

She sounded both disappointed and relieved, and I thought that perhaps she was not as invested in the success of the Project as she made out to be. Thoughts of retirement? Or...fear?

"I will," I said. "But for this, I need to step outside the prison-house. I need to go into their dream."

* * *

After what happened to my father, I had decided I no longer wanted my talent. The mutant genes in my brain could be switched off, at least some of them, and so I canceled the form I had signed in South Sudan and contacted the UN hospital in Istanbul. The procedure was too dangerous to be done at once, and I was to be hospitalized for a couple of weeks. I was alone; a fifteen-year-old with no visitors. They did something that resulted in bouts of nausea, blurred vision, and inability to remember Aramaic suffixes. I was set on continuing when I got a letter from my mother saying, essentially, that she never wanted to see me again. I checked myself out of the hospital that very day.

The thing is, the gene that they had switched off was one of the suite that the Project's subjects had had tampered with. In my brain, it clearly had played a different role: before my aborted procedure, I had been multilingual, rather than aphasic, and remained so after it. Even my Aramaic had come back. But what if the expression of this gene was somehow triggered or modified by the presence of others with a similar mutation? What if switching it back on would enable me to enter their shared dream-space without losing my ability to understand and speak human language? It was a slender hope, but it was all we had. The number of awake subjects dwindled every day. Rima was found curled up in her bed a couple of hours after our altercation. And if no one remained awake, who would I speak to, once I learned their language?

Having a mild anesthetic injected into my forearm, I seemed to float into some inchoate pink room, warm and cozy. But then I heard the sound of waves and smelled the fuggy rot of seaweed drying on the polluted shore.

***

This was supposed to be the last assignment I would accompany my parents on. I was growing up and my talents had drawn attention of various UN agencies. I had a place reserved for me in a very exclusive boarding school. But I had never been to Turkey before — or since.

Izmir, on the shores of the Aegean Sea, is one of the most beautiful cities of the region. But all I remember is the sluggish waves stirring the slime-covered pebbles and the rusty splatters of blood on the cobbles of Kemeralti.

The Circassian rebellion was winding down as we arrived, put down with efficient brutality by the government. It was our bad luck that a splinter group ran into us just as we were exiting the cab in front of the Karaca Hotel. They herded us away with curses and much waving of their antiquated rifles. They were speaking a sub-dialect of the Circassian, which I had not encountered before. It sounded like mint and wood varnish.

They blindfolded us and took us to a secret location. I heard them say its address several times. I also heard them say that we were not to be harmed, as they intended to trade us for a promise of safe passage to the Circassian Free Republic, which was to survive another month or so. I was not particularly worried, and neither were my parents, who had been in similar situations before. They knew that the way to handle the captors was to be as open and truthful as possible.

The window in the small room was barred, but the sash was raised to let air in, and it smelled of fish-rot. Didn't they realize that we could figure out our location without understanding their rapid-fire chat? Perhaps it was the intimation of our perfidy, rather than any real need to keep their paltry secret. Perhaps they subconsciously believed that the UN represented some promise of fairness in the world that was about to come crashing down around them.

They brought us tea and talked to my father in Turkish, which he had immediately told them he knew. They did not address my mother and me, us being mere women, and gave us white scarves to cover our hair, even though the rebellion was supposed to be secular and nationalistic, in opposition to Turkey's theocratic regime. Maybe that set me off. Or maybe it was just thoughtlessness. I don't remember.

One of them addressed their leader in Circassian, telling him they did not know how to get in touch with the UN Headquarters to inform them they had their people.

"It's in our phones, you fool!" I said, proud of my perfect pronunciation of his rough dialect. "Just dial! And do it quickly, I want out of this hole. They say Çeşme is a tourist town; sure doesn't look like one!"

I can still see the shock on their faces. And then the man who had spoken roughly dragged my father out of the room. He had lied to them, hadn't he? If his slip of a daughter could speak their obscure language so well, clearly the envoy and his family had prepared for this mission for a long time, ready to spy on the beleaguered freedom fighters. Who knew what schemes they were hatching with the hated government in Istanbul?

They did nothing to my mother and me. Perhaps they simply ran out of time, as the army raid that freed us happened less than an hour later. My father's body was found on the beach. They had cut out his tongue.

* * *

I felt exactly the same after the procedure, so I suspected it had not worked. Stella, harried as her stock of human guinea pigs dwindled every hour, wanted me to take a sleeping pill in the middle of the day, but I refused. Soporifics interfere with REM sleep. I listened to the tapes again, analyzing my one-sided interaction with Rima in audio and video. It struck me that her eyes did not seem to focus properly. One pupil was more dilated than the other.

I had a glass of red wine and fell asleep on my institutional bed.

I was walking on the rocky beach, or what seemed like a beach, only without any body of water to define its boundaries. Round stones, ranging in size from a bullet to an infant's head, slipped and tumbled under my bare feet. Some were furred with slimy weeds, others gave moistly, as if they were made of cheese. Sheets of fog whipped and danced around me, but there was no wind, and the air was as warm as blood. I followed the sound of breakers, but no matter how fast I tried to run or in what direction I turned, the surf was always one step ahead of me, too close but never close enough. Soon I realized that it was not a surf at all, but a multitude of people speaking together, their words blending into a meaningless noise.

A human shape loomed in the fog and advanced toward me. It was Rima, but something had happened to her. Her face had elongated into a muzzle like a dog's. She stared through me as she shambled by. A couple of others followed; I had seen them lying unresponsive in their hospital beds. They had all undergone some transformation, but it was different in each case. A man crawled on splayed flippers like an amphibian. Another hopped on a thick pad his legs had fused into. A woman cradled a big leech that suckled at her breast.

I opened my mouth to hail them and swallowed a wad of the warm fog that wormed its way into my gut, as comforting as my mother's milk, whose taste I had forgotten. There were no words anymore. The parasites had been expelled from my brain.

I dropped to my knees and started digging through the rocks, sorting through them and setting aside the right ones. It took a long time, except there was no time on the beach and no need to hurry, though hurry I did. Some of the stones were sharp-edged and broken, cutting my fingers, so that blood dripped into the hollow I made, and I was glad, hoping it would lure the right ones to the surface. There were stones beneath stones beneath stones. Some bit back when I separated them from their brethren. Some rolled away. Some licked me. And all the while, the susurrus of voices went on and on.

Finally, I had my pile. There was a yellow, porous stone like a chunk of bread with a little hole in the middle. There was a smooth, green-veined pebble. There was an agate that blinked at me with a black mildew spot. There was a bigger rock sparkling with an incrustation of pale crystals. And a couple of smaller ones, whose colors and shapes were as irrefutable as pain.

But I still missed one. I looked around in desperation when a man appeared out of fog.

It was my father. A glistening tentacle like that of a squid hung out of his mouth. He gave me the last stone and passed by me, disappearing into twilight.

* * *

"The Project has succeeded," I told Stella. She poured me another cup of tea and sat in the big armchair, staring at me. In the lifeless fluorescent light, I could see tiny lines on her taut cheeks.

"You mean, they are talking to aliens?"

I shrugged. My throat was raw, as if I had been screaming, which, apparently, I had. The oversweet tea did little to mask the metallic taste of blood and wet stone.

"Not sure that the aliens are still around. Perhaps. Perhaps they come to check on their handiwork from time to time."

"But that language…"

"It is not the aliens' language," I said. "Everything else is, but not this."

"What do you mean?"

I swallowed more hot liquid. I was parched.

"It is the original pre-human language. Or rather, the pre-human communication system. What we used when were like chimps, or songbirds, or bees. Before the implantation of the Chomsky module."

"You mean the aliens gave us language?"

"Sure. There is no way language could have evolved naturally. It is just too different, too complex. Too much of a piece. Could not have come about in incremental steps like everything else. Pre-human hominids had communication, sure, just like chimps and bonobos have today. Maybe more so, judging by how vocal your subjects are. But this was not language. And then the aliens came and tinkered with our brains and gave us the capacity for recursion and embedding and syntax. And everything else that has built the prison-house. Where we are today."

"Why?"

"I don't know," I lied.

"So," she said slowly, "language is a parasite. An alien parasite that has taken over and separated us from the rest of our biosphere. Made us what we are: strangers on our own planet."

I stared at her in amazement. I had clearly underestimated Major Stella.

"Yes," I said.

"But how is it that you are so different?"

I shrugged.

"I'm a mutant. Not that surprising, actually; mutations are ubiquitous. My Chomsky module is…improperly fitted, I guess, is a way to put it. We must all have a remnant of the pre-hominine communication system lodged in our brains, but the Chomsky module overrides it, presses it down into the darkness of dreams. But mine is unusually active. And to compensate, my Chomsky module also kicks into a hyperdrive, growing bigger, more active, more developed…"

"A parasite trying to suppress the host."

I nodded. Suddenly I just wanted to be alone. Talking to Stella was easier than any other conversation I had had in my life because the tastes and the smells and the textures of language had receded, leaving my mouth pristinely free to generate more words. More lies.

She got up.

"I need to write a report," she said. "You look tired…Sophia. Are you all right? Do you need anything?"

I shook my head. She patted my hand awkwardly, lingering at the door, as if expecting me to say something more, but I closed my eyes, faking fatigue. She left.

I got out of bed and went to the closet where I had hidden the piece of paper I had scribbled on after I woke up. Low-tech is guaranteed to be unique and irreplaceable. Not like computer files that can be infinitely copied, breeding more words in the world overflowing with language.

I had not lied to Stella about my being a mutant. This was my own best guess. But I had shaded the truth a little. I wondered whether she would figure it out herself.

If the aliens had seeded our brains with the Chomsky module, it must have been for a reason. They had wanted to communicate with us, or rather, with the creatures we would become. Could they foresee our spectacular technological progress? Had they planned on reaping the fruit of their little scheme millennia in advance? Why not? Who knew how long-lived they were?

Locking a bunch of clever primates in the prison-house of language and letting them play with this new toy until they discover nuclear fission, quantum computing, self-replicating neural nets. And then coming back to collect the inmates' output.

But whatever the original language programmed into the Chomsky module, it has branched and evolved into endless linguistic families, tongues, and dialects. The world has become a babbling cauldron of mutual incomprehension.

In such a world, one needs a translator.

A prison-guard to deliver orders to the inmates. A traitor.

I looked again at the wrinkled piece of paper — actually, an old receipt — on which I had scribbled the message I had received in the shared dream of the experimental subjects. The rocks I had dug up on the beach — those were words, the original ur-words of our creators speaking to us from outside the prison-house they had locked us in.

I tore the piece into two, and then again and again, until nothing remained but a handful of illegible fragments.

Publisher's Afterword

Stanisław Lem was born on 12 September 1921. This book was supposed to be a celebration of Lem's centenary in 2021. However, due to various difficulties, including a global pandemic, a war in Ukraine, and other problems more local to the publisher, the publication was delayed. It is now coming out in September 2022 — just in time for Lem's 101st birthday. Consider it as looking forward to Lem's second century, a challenge for us to continue grappling with his work that has lasting relevance to today's Anthropocene world.

I hope you have enjoyed this book. It is important to me and especially to the editor Elana Gomel. While I have read a bit of Lem's writing, he is a major influence and subject of study for her. This is the first book of what I hope will become a series. Please leave a review or comment online; it will help me work on more of these literary analysis books. Visit the Guardbridge Books web site to see more of our speculative fiction and non-fiction titles. http://guardbridgebooks.co.uk

—David Stokes, Publisher
Guardbridge Books
ST ANDREWS, SCOTLAND 2022

www.ingramcontent.com/pod-product-compliance
Lightning Source LLC
Chambersburg PA
CBHW072048110526
44590CB00018B/3086